Wartime Diary
of a
Maltese Boy

Wise Owl
PUBLICATION

Publishers: **Wise Owl** PUBLICATIONS, 59, Levels 1 & 2,
Main Street, Rabat RBT1012, Malta GC
Tel: 2145 3303   E-mail: wiseowl@maltanet.net
Website: www.wiseowlmalta.com

Wartime Diary of a Maltese Boy
First edition: MMVII
ISBN: 978-99932-92-71-5
Author: Laurence Mizzi
Copyright: © BIEB BIEB Enterprises Ltd.
Cover design: © **Wise Owl** PUBLICATIONS

*Special thanks go to Mr John A. Mizzi (editor "Malta at War") for proof reading
this publication.*

CONTENTS

To my grandchildren
Carole, Jamie and Colleen

INTRODUCTION

This volume from the pen of Laurence Mizzi will certainly be a most welcome addition to the literature in Maltese, especially that belonging to the autobiographical genre. It will also be welcomed as a book dealing with daily life as lived by the Maltese during the war, spanning a number of years embittered by hardship and suffering which inspired several poets but surprisingly few prose writers.

Those who lived through those momentous years have their own personal memories and recollections which, in spite of having a strong common element running through them, differ in details and perception. People might very well go through a common experience yet each has his or her own personal perception of the event so that when recounting the event each uses a particular style and a particular emphasis. In this respect Mizzi strikes the reader immediately as one whose writings are fluent and easy to read, without the slightest hint of pretentiousness or affectation, describing the cruelties and the sufferings resulting from the war as strengthening the morale of the people through a sense of solidarity and community feeling. Indeed throughout the book a note of humanity is never absent.

Two elements which also become evident as one reads the account are the sense of humour and the feeling of authenticity which flow effortlessly from the written word and which lend credibility to the story. The humorous element is not new; we have encountered it in some of Mizzi's short stories published since 1965 though that element was not as accentuated as in this volume which describe a childhood spent (or squandered away, some might think) in an environment very unlike that of the town where he was born. The humour serves here to temper the bitterness of life lived in constant threat of bombardment, starvation and disease.

As I was reading the manuscript what struck me most forcefully was the combination of realism and sincerity which runs through every page. Not only does Mizzi succeed in bringing back to life the past but also in retaining the modes of thinking as these were used in childhood. The picture he provides of himself is that of a child engrossed in the games, mostly inspired by the war, and continually engaged in those trivial pursuits which took up most of the waking hours of a refugee boy roaming the streets and alleys of the village or spending hours in the rock-cut shelters.

The incidents which Mizzi recounts have, without doubt, a documentary value but they are also of interest to the adult reader. Today's children, who have never lived through similar experiences, are more than likely to listen to the reminiscences of a person who has grown up during the war. "I was there" seems to be Mizzi's refrain on every page as those children listen with wide open ears.

In this book readers of every age will find something to stir their interest or to revive memories. Being some years older than Mizzi, I too find myself re-living memories as I read his book ...

It was quite some time ago that Laurence Mizzi was born in Vittoriosa (*Maltese:* Birgu); for some years he and I used to share the same office when in his post in the School Broadcasting Unit he used to write scripts which were very well received by audiences of every age. As a televiewer myself I remember being absorbed by his television programmes and by his genial personality. What I did not know at the time was that when I started my working life as a health inspector in Ħal Għaxaq, Laurence was a refugee boy in Gudja, a stone's throw away, and living through the experiences described in this book. As I read his book I could not help agreeing with his comments on the Gudja villagers' stout heart, their psychology and their outlook on life, traits which I saw matched at Ħal Għaxaq.

Most of the incidents recounted in the book were talked about in the streets of Ħal Għaxaq at the time so that I may say that these common experiences provide a link between the two of us. I am sure that people of my age will be able to compare their recollections with those of the author.

I heartily recommend this book to the reader; at the same time I would like to express my hopes that Mizzi will continue to regale us with more writings in the same charming style to enrich our youthful literature.

G. CASSAR PULLICINO

Ħal Balzan
8th August 1973

FOREWORD

Less than thirty years after the end of World War Two I decided to publish my "war memoirs." It had long been my wish to share with readers the experiences of a Maltese boy who lived through those terrible years of the "Second Great Siege". In 1939 we lived in the old maritime city of Birgu, which like the neighbouring Cospicua (*Maltese:* Bormla) and Senglea (*Maltese:* l-Isla) was very close to the Naval Dockyard, no doubt a prime target if and when war broke out.

Although at the time I was only eight years old I still have very vivid memories of the prevailing atmosphere in the late thirties when dark clouds were appearing on the horizon. Everybody then was talking about Hitler, Chamberlain and Mussolini, about war and gas attacks, evacuation and shelters. And when black out and curfew were introduced in May 1940 doubts turned into fear.

By 1939 the Government had already prepared elaborate plans for the evacuation of people living in the vicinity of the Dockyard and the harbour area. The man in charge of these plans was the Director of Education, Dr Albert V. Laferla (1887–1943). These plans included the twinning of towns to be evacuated with reception villages. Thus, for example, Bormla was twinned with Qormi, l-Isla with Żebbuġ and Siġġiewi, Birgu with Attard, Lija and Balzan … People were encouraged to follow these plans and move only to designated areas if war broke out. However in spite of all the precautions taken very few took any action and when on June 11, just hours after Italy's entry into the war on the side of Nazi Germany, Italian planes dropped the first bombs on the Island there

9

was a mass exodus from the danger zones with thousands heading towards unknown destinations in search of safety.

We were a bit luckier than most because only one day after bombs began to fall my extended family was able to move to a house in Gudja owned by the Society of Christian Doctrine (MUSEUM) thanks to Uncle Ġużeppi who was the superior of the village branch. For me and and no doubt, for those who were not yet in their teens, life in war time Malta was one huge adventure. Of course there were moments when life was unbearable: non-stop air attacks, loss of friends through enemy action, lack of everything including food, public transport practically non-existent ... However for us boys and girls there were compensations which more than made up for the suffering and pain which the people of Malta had to endure between 1940 and 1942.

This modest volume is all about this or, to be more precise, about my own personal experiences. Some are perhaps unique; others no doubt are shared by those, now in their seventies, who grew up and "matured" during the years when our Island home had to endure, in the words of Lord Gort, Governor of Malta, "the most concentrated bombing attacks in the history of the world". (Philip Vella: *Malta Blitzed but not Beaten*, p. 121) and then starvation which almost forced the British to surrender the Island.

I would like to thank the late Ġużè Cassar Pullicino who wrote the introduction to the original in Maltese (1973). My thanks go also to the playwright and author, the late Ġino Muscat Azzopardi who provided most of the footnotes based on the diary of events which he kept during the war and to author and historian Dr Charles J. Boffa for his assistance.

My special thanks go to my lifelong friend Prof J.M. Falzon who once again accepted to translate the original Maltese text of *Dħaħen tal-Gwerra*. His interest and constructive criticism are also gratefully acknowledged.

15 August 2006   Laurence Mizzi

CHAPTER 1

The gathering storm

One Saturday in the first weeks of the summer of 1939 a group of boys between the ages of eight and ten could be seen on the steps of the Oratory of the Holy Crucifix in Birgu, one of the two small churches in the vicinity of the parish church of St Lawrence. The purpose of the meeting was to demonstrate their loyalty to the "general" whom they had just elected from among themselves and at the same time to present him with some gifts. There was a gift from every boy: a holy medal from one, a cheap bracelet from another, a handful of naval brass buttons presumably torn off a sailor's uniform and so on. The buttons were put to immediate use; the "general" there and then inserted them into his shirt. The "general" happened to be myself and I still have some of those gifts. I confess that up to this very day I can offer no explanation as to why those boys had chosen me as their "general – perhaps that was because I was the youngest or, equally plausible because I was the shortest of the lot. The matter, however, need not concern the reader unduly; the important point for the gist of the story is the tendency of young children to imitate the behaviour of their elders. The children were not playing the sort of games popular in those days, like catch or marbles but a childish imitation of war.

In those days the newspapers regularly carried the latest news about Hitler and the Nazis, Mussolini, and the events taking place in Europe. As can be imagined I could not have an understanding of what was going on at the time; yet, even at the tender age of eight or thereabouts I had a kind of vague feeling that something was wrong, a feeling reinforced by the multitude of people praying in churches, the pilgrimages and processions with holy statues. The distribution of gas masks to the population and the constant reminders on the Rediffusion[1] about the proper use of the masks should an attack take place heightened that feeling in me. Still, in spite of the gathering clouds and the threat of a gas attack, we children could still find enjoyment in our childish war games.

It was agreed that each of us would buy a paper bag and contribute a halfpenny (today's equivalent would be about a cent). We each cut two eyeholes in the paper bag and put it over our heads. We made our way to the bastions where we collected handfuls of dust before going back to St Lawrence Square to chase one another, throwing handfuls of dust at children and passers-by; the dust, naturally, was meant to represent a gas attack, an eventuality which was then rampant in everyone's mind. In fact only a few days before, in that same square, a simulation of a gas attack had been mounted during which people had been ordered to stay indoors while military lorries rumbled through the narrow streets spreading clouds of fine dust which was thought to be similar to gas. We children, along with, I imagine, the entire population of the town watched the whole show from behind window shutters and balconies. Our version of the gas attack did not last for long as we were told off in no uncertain terms by our victims.

Another popular pastime for us was to sleep under the dining table. People were advised by the authorities to pile up mattresses on the sturdiest table in the house to absorb the impact of falling slabs should the building suffer damage during an air raid. At our age, the whole routine was regarded as great entertainment and one can imagine how we enjoyed every moment Often enough the entertainment was brought to a sudden halt by a couple of slaps and then to a deep sleep, in my case only to be broken by bad dreams about the German attacks.

While these childish pranks helped to pass the time for us youngsters, clear evidence that the impending war was coming closer and closer could no longer be ignored. The "Black Outs"[2] were being introduced regularly; this meant that at certain hours all lights were to be put out or completely concealed in such a way that not one chink of light could be detected from outside. For us, the "Black Out" was, as one would expect, another source of amusement for inventive young minds, but our games would be halted as soon as one of the wardens who were meant to see that the "Black Out" was being observed would come round and sternly warn us that lights were to be extinguished if we wanted to steer clear of trouble. Scared as we were of these wardens our merriment would stop abruptly and a worried look would take the place of our smiles and laughter.

The dreaded word "war" was on everybody's lips; yet I am not sure that the people at large could understand the import of it. Take me, for instance. In my imagination war meant that enemy warships would break into the Grand Harbour, point their guns at the walls of the towns and raze every building to the ground. Airplanes never came into the scheme of things. In those days there were very few airplanes about and I remember how we used to stop whatever we were doing every time an airplane flew overhead so that we could watch the unusual sight, very much as in our days we would do if a flying saucer appeared in the sky.

In spite of this general lack of understanding of a state of war, preparations were under way in many areas, even though as it turned out later these preparations were found to be in most cases inadequate and misguided. Families were asked to go to the local school to be issued with gas masks[3] and to have some training in their use. Masks came in different forms and sizes; even babies had their own specially made versions. The distribution of gas masks was another source of entertainment for us but for old people, who had breathing problems already, the masks were a source of added difficulty. These old people could never have imagined the tribulations that were coming their way in their old age.

The expected gas attacks never materialized but the heavy air bombardment did and as the authorities made their preparations, irrelevant and inadequate as they were, the ordinary housewife began to make her own arrangements. Hoarding became the order of the day; shopkeepers, especially grocers, had their shelves cleared in next to no time. Housewives filled pillowcases and boxes with sugar, soap, matches and tinned milk. Such hoarding is difficult to imagine these days when there is such an abundance of goods for sale.

There was at the same time a lot of talk about evacuation to the villages. In those days if you happened to own a place in one of the villages you were lucky and you could put your mind at rest – you would be safe for the duration of the war. I remember my family renting a house in Qormi; to this day I remember the feeling of excitement and expectation on that Sunday afternoon when I went with my aunt to have a look at the place. Thoughts were running through my mind: "If there has to be a war for us to move there, may it break out soon." We did not stay at that place for long as my parents could not afford to rent two houses and so decided to vacate that house. That gave me the idea that peace brings its own problems no less than war.

People were like that in those days; at one instant they felt

14

terrified by the thought of the destruction that was in store for them, then they would read or hear the latest statements made by politicians (with hindsight I know that one of these politicians was the peace loving Chamberlain[4]) and believe that everything would solve itself out and there would be no war after all. All uncertainty was abruptly stopped when on Monday, the tenth of June 1940 the Italian dictator Benito Mussolini[5] announced that Italy had formed a pact with Germany and the country was therefore at war with Great Britain. I clearly recollect some of the events of that fateful day: the most vivid memory is that of my going to the main square of Birgu (Birgu) at about six or seven and seeing a crowd of people who had gathered to listen to the latest news on the public Rediffusion set. At the end of the news bulletin I could hear people mutter, "Italy is now at war; that means that we are at war too." At that time such a statement did not mean much to me or to those of my age but it was not to take long for us to understand the full import of living in a country which was at war.

Notes and references

1. Rediffusion Relay System started its operations in Malta in 1935 following an agreement with the British Government. Subscribers were provided with two services: one channel broadcast the BBC World Service and the second relayed broadcasts from other countries including Italy (*Broadcasting: a Commitment to Pluralism*, Department of Information, 1990). Government made daily contacts with the people before and during the war by means of Rediffusion loudspeakers which had been installed in squares of towns and villages thus enabling people to listen to news and official communications at certain times of the day.

2. "Black Out" and curfew regulations came into force in May 1940, that is just before Italy entered the war.

3. Gas masks were distributed during the first months of 1940. Distribution of gas masks was mainly carried out in school premises but there were also large vans stopping at various points in towns and villages to

demonstrate their use. Manning the vans were schoolteachers, health inspectors and members of the Police Force, all of whom had attended courses about the correct use of the masks and could now pass on that knowledge to the people. Adults and children wearing masks were made to sit in the vans while gas was released in weak doses. (CJ Boffa)

4. The Rt. Hon. (Arthur) Neville Chamberlain (1869-1940) was British Prime Minister from 1937 to 1940. He made great efforts to maintain peace by trying to avoid confrontation. Some historians argue that his appeasement policy did much to encourage Hitler's ambitions and in the end was the cause of the outbreak of the War in 1939 by which time Germany had had enough time to put the country on a war footing, being in fact far more prepared than Britain and her Allies.

5. Benito Mussolini, the Italian dictator, declared war on the Allies in a speech delivered from the balcony of Palazzo Venezia in Rome on June 10, 1940. Italy was declared to be in a state of war as from midnight between the 10th and the 11th of that month. Mussolini's speech was enthusiastically received by the immense crowd assembled in the great square stretching before the palace.

CHAPTER 2

The storm breaks

Tuesday, June 11: It was getting on to seven and we had scarcely got out of bed before the morning's silence was broken by the plaintive wail of the siren.[1] We were five children in the family and we looked at each other as if to try and understand what was going on. My mother was no wiser; none of us knew what message the wailing siren was trying to convey and much less what we were supposed to do. Our bafflement, however, soon vanished when we heard gunfire and a series of explosions and things became suddenly clear when my aunt, who was on her way to mass, appeared and in a voice which betrayed her terror cried, "The aeroplanes are dropping bombs!" The next instant all of us dived under the dining table and waited for the din to stop. I have no recollection as to the duration of this air raid, the first of the hundreds to follow. I remember, however, that later that morning there were other air raids and my aunt, curious as ever, decided that she would see with her own eyes what an air raid was like. She half opened one of the shutters in the balcony and leaned out to have a look.

At that very instant one of the newly appointed wardens, who was wearing an armband with the letters SC (Special Constable) and was patrolling the street caught sight of her and shouted sternly, "What are you doing in that balcony?

17

Have you come out to see Saint Roque?" (In those days, at Birgu, there was the annual procession held on the feast day of that saint when a statue representing Saint Roque was carried through the streets of the town.) "Get inside at once and close the shutters!" My aunt, taken aback at the warden's warning, did as she was, in no uncertain terms, told to do by the man with the armband, who I imagine, knew as little about modern warfare as my aunt did. If he knew, I am sure he would have taken shelter instead of strutting about with the self importance that an armband can give you, even though he might have felt perfectly safe under his steel helmet.

We spent that first day of the war indoors. It seems that everybody did the same as unlike on a normal day the streets were deserted. When darkness fell and the family had recited the rosary as usual but with the addition of some prayers for peace, we all went to bed – under the dining table. I remember that on that occasion nobody was in the mood for pleasantries; it had taken us only a few hours to learn that war was no childish joke. To make matters worse my father, a Dockyard employee, did not come home that evening and he had to take the night shift instead; that was precisely when the family more than at any other time was in need of the father to be with his family. I remember how terrified I was that night. It was not simply a fear of being killed or falling into the hands of the enemy; it was rather a kind of undefined anxiety resulting from uncertainty about what the morrow had in store for us. That night, as we went to bed, we must have had a premonition that life as we had lived it up to that day would change for all of us, even if none of us, thank God, could imagine at that moment the hardship we were destined to go through.

I do not remember how we passed that night except that the five of us children slept under the table in the belief that we were safe. If I dreamt that night, I can imagine what dreams

I had. What I am sure about is that at dawn my mother woke us up: "Get up and get dressed at once so that we can leave…" "Where are we going?" I asked. "We are going to Gudja to stay with Uncle."

Gudja is one of the smallest and least known villages of Malta and to us children the name meant little or nothing. My uncle was the head of the local branch of the Society of Christian Doctrine (the MUSEUM), and a few weeks before war broke out he had taken us to that village on the occasion of the First Holy Communion in the community, an event which, as is well known, is locally celebrated with great fervour. The word soon spread in the neighbourhood that we were moving to Gudja and that a private bus would be calling for us and before you knew it we had several relatives, close and not so close, at our door begging to go with us. My uncle, who happened to be involved in Operation Evacuation, was quite happy to oblige and by the time the private bus stopped at our door, there was quite a number of people, all carrying necessities, waiting for a lift. There was little time to lose and within minutes we were all on board ready to drive away. There was practically everybody there: my uncle and aunt and their mother, my grandmother; our family, five children and my mother; another aunt with three children one of whom a baby of a few days; my father's cousins, my godfather, two elderly sisters and Uncle Wenzu. As the bus started moving we made the sign of the cross as we left behind us the town in which we were born and to which we were closely attached.

Come to think of it … in the Great Siege of 1565 it was the villagers who left behind their homes and sought shelter inside the walls of Birgu and now, four hundred years later, the opposite has come to pass, people abandoning the towns and seeking refuge in the villages, away from the dockyards and the harbours, from the destruction and death that would be dealt to the towns. Now things were different in other ways, too; the enemy was not launching attacks by sea or land but from the skies, just as on occasion a plague of locusts attacks fields and crops. Once again we were in for a hard time. In 1565 the people could find refuge behind the town walls but now there was no shield to ward off attacks from the air as there were no rock cut shelters as yet. That was how we left behind us our homes, which next to members of one's family, are one's dearest possessions and parted from friends we had known from childhood and some of whom we were destined never to see again. As we proceeded on our way we could see buses, trucks and horse drawn carts, piled high with belongings, all moving in the same direction, from the towns to the villages. The evacuation of the towns around the harbours had begun.

Notes and references

1. The first air raid took place on June 11 at 6.50 a.m. During that first raid bombs were dropped on Ħal Far aerodrome, Fort Bengħisa and Birżebbugia causing only minor damage. At 8.15 a.m. of the same day a wave of ten Italian aircraft dropped bombs on Corradino, Porte des Bombes, Pietà and Sa Maison. A number of buildings were destroyed and some persons were killed, among them a woman from Pietà, a certain Antonia Farrugia, who was probably the first victim of the war. Six soldiers from the Royal Malta Artillery (the RMA) were killed as they manned a gun in Fort St Elmo. This second attack lasted for about twenty minutes. An hour later there was an air raid alert but the enemy planes turned back without attacking the Island. On that first day of the war, there were eight air raid alerts in all.

CHAPTER 3

We move to Gudja

I have little or, at best a very vague recollection of the trip
from Birgu to Gudja; all I remember is that it was a long
time before we got to our destination. I remember that in
front of us and behind us were hundreds of evacuees, like us
making their way out of the dangerous harbour area. I seem
to remember, too, passing by the half-built parish church of
Paola (*Maltese:* Raħal Ġdid), a town which I had previously
been to on a number of occasions. That morning, as we
trudged up the square, I was struck as never before by the
immense proportions of that temple. (The church was far
from completion at the time and it took a full twenty years
before that great structure got its finishing touches in 1960.)
On reaching Gudja we made a bee-line for the building which
housed the Society of Christian Doctrine (MUSEUM) and
which had now become for us a providential new home. The
house was no palace: an entrance hall, a room to one side,
a staircase and on the first floor a fairly large room which
served as a chapel, and from which a spiral stairway led to the
rooftop. Behind the house was a large yard with three rooms
and a pigsty. The three rooms in the yard were already taken
up by two families from Raħal Ġdid. Looking back today I
can never stop wondering how so many people – twenty in all

– with the youngest a baby of a few days and the oldest aged some seventy years could manage to live in that house. And that is without counting the two families living in the rooms in the yard! Try to imagine that!

The reader may here ask, "And what about bedding and other furniture?" We simply laid blankets on the floor; summer was still with us so that, at least, was not a problem. When we looked up and saw the wooden beams and the roof slabs instead of stars and the open sky we felt we had much to thank God for.

Although our country is very small and there are no distances to speak of, I remember vividly, as if it were yesterday, how I was struck by the many differences between Gudja and my home town of Birgu. For instance most houses in the village consisted of a ground floor and therefore the streets were brighter and sunnier than in Birgu where streets were narrower and where houses were generally built on three or four floors. With the exception of the main road, which was asphalted, all the streets of Gudja were covered with a thick layer of dust. Most of the villagers went about barefooted and their clothing was not like the sort you saw in Birgu; women wore dark clothes with skirts reaching down to their ankles. As for men you could not see one wearing a jacket; instead they wore flannel shirts and Malta weave trousers turned up at the ankles. Most of the men wore caps. The boys wore tight knee-length trousers held up with suspenders crossed at the back. The girls wore pigtails and their skirts covered the knees. Another thing which made an impression on me was the fact that the front door of every house was kept closed but with the key in place – a practice which I think survives to this day in some of the more isolated villages of Malta and Gozo.

We had left Birgu in a hurry without having the time to get hold of some utensils and foodstuff to carry us through the day, so that the first thing we did on arriving at our destination was to pay a visit to the grocer whose shop was right opposite the house which was going to be our home. We bought plates, cutlery, buckets, brooms and things of that sort and then, of course, the foodstuff: bread and butter, cheese, oil, spaghetti and similar necessities. By the time we finished I think we must have cleared the shop of every commodity. I remember the woman at the shop was one of those sturdy villagers, with her hair tied into a bun and with a deep raucous voice that, in some curious way, sounded kind in our ears.

During our first evening in the village I remember stepping into the parish church and staring in amazement at the sky blue dome covered with silver stars. The silence that reigned in the church heightened the mysterious atmosphere of that temple; the war raging around the world, the village which was all new to me, the silence inside the church were all part of the mystery. On leaving the church and on the way to my new home my eyes were taking in every detail, every new sight such as the curtains made of stringed beads hanging in most shop doors. As the evening wore on women came out of their houses and sat on their doorsteps doing some of the housework, patching up clothes, peeling potatoes, reciting the rosary. This, I learnt later, was a habit common to most villages; the memory of that street scene is still with me and somehow brings up in me a feeling of contentment and serenity. As I walked along with my mother the villagers recognized us for what we were and I could hear them mutter under their breath "There go the refugees!" I remember that during that first evening there was an air raid but the action was on the other side of the island and the explosions and gun fire could be heard only faintly in the distance.

That first day passed uneventfully but the night that followed was different; it was a night that I would not easily forget in the years to come. It was not because it was the first night away from home that made it so unforgettable; it was because of a tiny insect which produced a noise vastly out of proportion to its size. When we arrived in the village my brother and I made friends with one of the local boys, Ġużi by name, roughly my age or a bit older, who fully deserved the reputation of being the most mischievous youngster in the whole of Gudja. On that day Ġużi gave us a cicada and instructed us to cage it in an empty milk tin and feed it on bits of tomato. "You'll be surprised at the way it sings", he told us. My brother Josie and I had never before seen or heard a cicada and we immediately proceeded to follow his instructions and placed the tin with the cicada in the hall. As the evening grew darker and night set in, the cicada began its performance and Ġuzi's words were fully borne out.

My brother and I listened intently for as long as we could keep our eyes open until we dropped off into a sound sleep. The older people in the house trying to snatch some sleep on the blankets laid on the floor were not quite as happy with the performance. As we all know older people do not fall asleep as easily as youngsters especially on their first night in a strange place where instead of comfortable beds they had to make do with a blanket spread out on a hard stone floor. The cicada's night long performance certainly did not improve matters. No one seemed to be able to discover the hiding place of the cicada and at least until morning broke no one suspected that my brother and myself were responsible for the performance. But truth will out, as they say, and before long we were the target of all those who had spent a sleepless night. Even my mother became the target of the inmates' rage and, though normally very tolerant and calm in the face of our misbehaviours, she now became furious and made us ferret out the cicada and get rid of it. The cicada was now in the same boat as us – homeless. For quite some time in our room my brother and I were sniffling and sobbing – a performance to match that of the cicada.

The public health authorities were understandably very concerned about the possible hazards, like epidemics, which could result from the overcrowding of living quarters which the influx of refugees brought about. Their concern was made greater when , as I described before, sanitary facilities were primitive or non-existent; the public sewage system had not yet reached most of the villages and the majority of homes did not have running water. Villagers got their water from the public stand pipes and from wells which were found in most houses.

I have hazy recollections of inspections being carried out in various houses which had received refugees so that the situation would be kept under control or at least improved in some way. There was one inspection which I remember clearly. A man from the Health Department knocked on the door and announced that he was a sanitary inspector and that he wanted to speak to all the persons living in the house. We all came down into the yard and stood in a circle and listened. I cannot quite remember what he spoke about but I suppose he must have spoken about the importance of hygiene in the place to avoid the risks of catching some disease. I have no doubt that the official's little talk contained large doses of good and useful advice but I have many doubts about the extent to which his recommendations were put into practice by the attentive listeners. I remember that before he left the inspector said, "One other thing! No one is allowed to keep animals in the house. I am sure you haven't brought with you any pets, is that right?" "No, we haven't" replied in unison the listeners including my mother. "Yes, we have!" I shouted in my innocence. And as I was about to reveal some details about a few rabbits which we had brought along with us and which were now running around in the pigsty, my mother, in a way which was very unusual for her slapped me in the face and whispered, "Shut up or the inspector will hear you".

"I beg your pardon, what did you say?" the inspector was quick to ask my mother.

"Nothing", my mother was equally quick to answer.

As soon as the official left everybody heaved a sigh of relief. My mother, backed by others, turned on me and seething with anger shouted, "You almost landed me with a fine!"

"Why did you interfere, you busybody?" chimed in Karmena, a distant relative of the family who was never at a loss for words.

"See that you don't do that again", said another.

"But isn't it true that we have got rabbits in the house?" I said, not willing to go down without a fight.

"That's none of your business", the three shouted in chorus.

"But I shouldn't tell lies, should I?" said I, resolved to have the last word.

"No, you shouldn't tell lies but you shouldn't say anything either", they said.

I felt sorry not because of the telling off I got from them as much as for the conviction that I had that I was right and they were wrong; I had been taught to always tell the truth and now I was being scolded for doing just that.

Shortly after living in that house for some weeks my father and mother decided to move to another place, Gejtu's house. Here I would like to say that the authorities in those days were putting the pressure on those villagers who owned a large house to take in refugees from the harbour areas. For various reasons, rightly or wrongly, not all villagers were willing to do so; perhaps the idea of sharing one's house with strangers is not to everybody's taste, especially so when these strangers came from a background which was very different from theirs.

Gejtu was a dockyard worker and it was at the dockyard that my father got to know him. I cannot say now whether it was my father who first broached the idea of having our family moving to Gejtu's house or whether it was the other way round. There is also the possibility that since the authorities could make you open your doors to strangers Gejtu thought that it would be better to pre-empt the authorities by letting into his house someone he knew to be the right sort. What is certain is that my father and mother, both in the prime of their life – my father was 39 and my mother a couple of years younger – with five children aged from one year to nine years could not live in the MUSEUM house for more than a few weeks, in overcrowded conditions. I imagine that the possibility of having a room to themselves and sharing the house with only one other family was too attractive to let go by.

And so we were now living in Gejtu's house. For us children the move was heaven-sent; we had now more room to move around in. True, we found that now we had lost a part of our freedom as we were constantly admonished by our parents to be quiet and to behave all the time as otherwise "Gejtu would drive us out of the house". I still have a mental picture of that house. It was a typical village house: you went in through the front door into a fairly large yard around which were built a few rooms. We had one of those rooms, possibly the largest in the house, which when compared to our previous accommodation was very spacious. As they say, it's all a question of relativity, and we were very happy with our new quarters. For us children it was a godsend. Gejtu owned a few fields in the neighbourhood and used to be a bird hunter and he often took me and my brother Josie with him when setting out on one of his hunting expeditions. In addition his children were roughly about the same age as ours or perhaps a bit older and we soon made friends.

This happy interlude, however, was not to last for long. My mother fell victim to rheumatism and was often in great pain; she could hardly walk as the condition affected her ankles badly.

Moving from one end of the room to another meant crawling on all fours like a baby. Forty years ago you could not find the wide variety of medicines which we have got used to these days when for every ailment there is the appropriate remedy. To make matters worse, there was a war on and medicines, like everything else, were not always readily available. Living in Gudja made the situation even more difficult as the village did not have a pharmacy. To make up for that a pharmacist from the nearby village of Luqa used to go through the streets of Gudja twice a week in a horse-drawn cab stocked with the medicines available at the time. As the cab rumbled through the streets the pharmacist would blow a car horn to inform the locals of his arrival. Now and then he would stop and a crowd would surround the cab with doctors' prescriptions in hand.

Gradually, my mother got better and for the moment it seemed that our troubles were over. But there was more to come for another problem arose, a problem for which no solution has ever been found, that of jealousy. Gejtu's wife, some years older than my mother, suddenly began to suspect that her husband was casting his eyes elsewhere, precisely at my mother. I was too young then to make heads or tails of the situation and to this day I cannot say whether her suspicions were justified or whether Gerit, for that was her name, was by nature suspicious and the situation whereby you had strangers in the house was such as to fire her imagination. Whatever the reason Gerit, soon started behaving strangely. At first she began to sulk, then she started looking crossly at members of my family and would avert her eyes when one of us crossed her path. Then she became aggressive. Gejtu continued to behave normally at the beginning but then, I imagine under pressure from his wife, he started copying his wife in his relations with us.

Even though I was very young I could sense the change in his behaviour. Where he used to be friendly with us children, he would now pass by without saying a word; no longer would he take us to his fields or on his hunting trips. It was as if he had never known or met us, as if we were complete strangers. I have never discovered what his relations to my father were; I would like to think that when the two were at their place of work, or on their way there and out of sight of Gerit, Gejtu behaved differently and that the two men got on well together. But the upshot was inevitable: we had to move out and find another place to live. It was bad enough that we were at war with Italians and Germans and we could ill afford to wage a domestic war at the same time. My father and mother came to the conclusion that they had no choice but to return to the MUSEUM house. Luckily for us the house was not as crowded as when we left. Aunt Saverina, her three children, Uncle Wenzu, my godfather Toni and two of the latter's relatives had moved to other premises and therefore when we found ourselves back in St Mary Street there was more elbow room which was soon to be marginally diminished with the birth of another brother.

CHAPTER 4

The first months

The simplicity with which life was lived in Gudja attracted me like a magnet; surrounded as the village was with fields it made an immediate impact on me. It was totally different from the Birgu I knew, where you could not see a patch of soil anywhere and where you had to walk quite some distance, towards the Capuchin Friary, in Kalkara, to see some open countryside. Gudja was the opposite – wherever you looked you saw fields stretching as far as the eye could see. The neighbourhoods went by different names: Dawra Ddur, il-Ħanija, il-Ħofra, iż-Żebbuġa, Ta' Loretu, il-Karwija ... all of them containing fields.

Of course fields were not there just to be looked at ... Within a few days of our settling there, Ġużi, who had by now become my closest friend, asked me and my brother Josie to go with him to his uncle's fields so that, as he said, we could pick a few figs. Needless to say that was an offer we could not refuse and the three of us were soon on our way out of the village and walking in eager anticipation of what was in store for us. At one point Ġużi stopped and said, "This is my uncle's field. You can go in and help yourselves." That was the signal we were waiting for and, before you could bat an eyelid, the three of us were under a fig tree the branches of which were groaning with loads of delicious figs. As we helped ourselves I remember saying to myself how lucky we were to be able to eat to our hearts' content and how different things were from the Birgu I knew. How lucky to have a friend whose uncle had a field like this!

I was congratulating myself on my good fortune, especially the fact that we had moved to this place, when I caught sight of a man running towards us brandishing a hoe and bellowing, "So it's you! I have caught you, you lot of ...! You've ruined my tree! You'll pay for it if I lay my hands on you!" My brother and I were naturally surprised and looked at one another, not quite knowing what to do next. At first we thought that the man had somehow made a mistake and took us for someone else but we were not left in doubt much longer when we saw Ġużi dropping the figs and scrambling over the rubble walls with the agility of a monkey, running as fast as he could and shouting, "Run! Don't let Toni catch you!" In my innocence I could only reply, "But isn't the field your uncle's?"

"Shut up and run!" was all Ġużi could say. We were lucky that day to have got away without any serious trouble. From that day onwards we stopped listening to Ġużi's promptings and soon learnt who were the real owners of each field in the neighbourhood.

The countryside, now, as then, holds a certain fascination for me; one of my greatest pleasures is to walk along the country lanes observing the peasants working in their fields: ploughing, sowing, reaping, harvesting, watering and weeding. In my childhood the sight of farmers working their patch filled me with a sort of inner contentment; now that many years have passed I still experience the same feeling. That was the main reason which made me fall in love with the village of Gudja. However, in this kind of idyllic state there was one thing which jarred: the absence of a public sewage system. The good people of Gudja, of course, could not be blamed for that. Indeed up to a few years ago there were still a number of villages in Malta and Gozo which had to manage without a sewage system; Gudja was one of them. Many of the houses were provided with a cesspit but the place we were living in did not have this amenity with the result that we had to carry buckets every day to a public pit in a field some distance away. We took this daily task by turns and when my turn came I remember I used to be very embarrassed and curse the day when Mussolini decided to get us involved in the war.

Another chore which irked me no end was the daily carrying of buckets of water from the public standpipe to our new home, especially as this robbed me of hours of playing around. At certain times of the day you could see dozens of people waiting their turn to fill their buckets and forming what to me seemed like a never ending queue made up mostly of women, children of all ages and sometimes men carrying a variety of containers, pails, jars, jugs and basins which came in all shapes, colours and sizes.

At about this time Gudja began to receive a number of regiments for whom tents were set up on the outskirts of the village. One can easily imagine how the presence of so many soldiers fired the imagination of us youngsters. I remember how all the boys soon learnt the English expressions to run up to the soldiers to beg for Egyptian coins; I know now that some of the regiments had just retreated from Egypt. From that starting point it was an easy step to learn how to beg for other things besides cash as, for example, cigarettes and chocolate.

The *Hampshires*[1] was one of the regiments stationed at Gudja; the crest on their caps showed the head of a tiger. Each of us boys had their favourite soldier; in my case this was a sergeant, George, who was known to his mates as "Queenie". He was still a young lad, although to us children he appeared to be a mature man; he was a likeable person, with a very fair, freckled face and the kindest person you could think of. I would wait for him every day near Żeża's wine shop and at about half past four he would drop in for a glass of wine and buy me a bottle of lemonade while talking to me. I think he treated me as if I was a grown-up lad rather than a child of nine. I can understand now how patient he must have been to take such pains to carry on a conversation with me especially as my English, then, was extremely limited. I believe that the presence of so many Englishmen around in those days was a godsend in more ways than one. One of the benefits stemming from the situation was that we had plenty of opportunities to practise the English language and I feel sure that in a few months we learnt that language more than we could have done in two or three years at school. As a matter of fact, many of the soldiers picked up a large number of Maltese words and phrases; as expected the first words which they learnt were the Maltese for "girl", "sweet", "I love you" and similar expressions together with some words which are not printable in a book like this. Occasionally you would find a soldier who managed to get a good command of the Maltese language in a short while. I know, now, that the socializing of children with adult strangers is not something that one should encourage but as far as I am concerned, and here I only speak for myself, I cannot recollect any instance of improper conduct on the part of those soldiers.

During the first months of the war, that is the time I am writing about, life had more or less returned to normal.[2] Air raids appeared to be half-hearted and infrequent and several refugee families left the village, to return to the towns. I remember one occasion when I went with my uncle and aunt to Birgu, some five months into the war, and saw deserted streets such that Birgu looked like a ghost town; no people could be seen and you could hear the sound of your footsteps echoing back from the walls. Weeds were sprouting through the cracks between the flagstones. One scene struck me particularly: the sight of a number of people sleeping under St Helen's Gate at Bormla; it was thought in those days that the safest place to be during an air raid was beneath an arch or in a tunnel.

The fact that for the first months the air raids were comparatively mild was a blessing in disguise for it provided the population with some breathing space during which those preparations which should have been in place long before could be carried through. It was during these first few months that bomb-proof, rock cut shelters began to be dug in earnest.[3] Like other children, I used to spend hours watching the miners wielding massive picks to dig into the hard stone inch by inch and occasionally using dynamite to blast the rock. The shelters used to have two entrances with a distance of about twenty metres between them. The miners used to start digging the shelter from both ends and when the two tunnels met half way through you could hear people talking excitedly as if some great event had taken place. Indeed one could say that there was more than enough reason to rejoice at the completion of every shelter; the shelters were the catacombs of the twentieth century and the people were seeking shelter not from the fury of the heathen but from the might of the enemy who had sworn to exterminate them. The expected devastation of the island did not materialize during the first months of the war and one can safely say the people soon got used to the Italian air raids and could almost forget that there was a war raging at the time.

For instance, it was a commonly held belief that the Italian pilots were more scared of the Maltese defences than the other way round. I recollect that a neighbour of ours who owned a wireless set (a rarity in those days), in defiance of regulations in force at the time, used to tune in to the Italian pilots' conversations while they were flying over Malta during routine bombing missions. This neighbour was fond of recounting how on such occasions he could hear the alarmed voices of the pilots over the radio exclaiming "*Mamma mia!*" and, as Maltese would tend to do on similar occasions, invoke a myriad of saints when they saw the barrages of anti-aircraft fire through which they had to fly. According to our neighbour, the most popular of the saints invoked was San Gennaro who seemed to have a special place in pilots' hearts. After listening to such stories people began to take the Italian air raids lightly, often going as far as treating the whole business as if it was all a joke. Children in Gudja had a jingle which ran,

> *Air Raid Warning, Air Raid Pas(t),*
> *Mussolini il-fartas;*
> *Xeħet Bomba fuq Ħal Luqa,*
> *Qatel fenek u għattuqa.*

and which can be roughly translated as

> Air Raid Warning, Air Raid Pas(t)
> Baldheaded Mussolini
> Dropped a bomb on Luqa
> Killing a rabbit and a hen.

In general there seemed to be a sense of optimism in the air; I remember hearing about people betting that the war was about to end. Even as a child I realized that since there were those who were making such bets there must also be a number who were certain of a different outcome and were betting on a long drawn out conflict. At the end of the day, it was the latter who were to be proved right; the war had barely started!

Notes and references

1. The *Hampshires* landed in Malta on February 23, 1941. They were quartered in Gudja, Żurrieq and Ħal Safi. "A" Company was stationed

in Gudja and was charged with the defence of the Hal Safi end of the aerodrome as well as the southern coast. Probably, of all regiments in Malta, the *Hampshires* was the one which saw most action. The regiment left Malta on March 30, 1943 and proceeded to Egypt. During their stint in Malta the regiment suffered 12 killed and 27 wounded. (*Regimental History, The Royal Hampshire Regiment, Vol 3*)

2. After the first few weeks, attacks by Italian aircraft began to be taken lightly by the population at large as these began to be seen as ineffective. In fact, on many occasions the Italian planes would drop their bombs into the sea and turn back before actually reaching our shores. By the day the Italians stopped coming to Malta they had chalked up 1787 sorties.

3. The first rock-cut shelters were excavated at the Dockyard in 1939. Later on, in 1940, shelters were constructed in the Three Cities and in the vicinity of the airfields. (CJ Boffa)

CHAPTER 5

The *Luftwaffe* strikes

It was the January 16, 1941, a Thursday, I remember. At about two in the afternoon an air raid warning was treated by most people as a routine and trivial interruption, not to be taken too seriously: a few shots in the distance and the interruption would be over, as usual. It did not take us long to realize that this time it was a different game altogether. Explosion followed explosion and for a long interval it sounded as if all hell was let loose. The enemy aircraft were flying low, skimming rooftops, with the sound of their engines adding to the din. Even from the depths of the shelter we were in we could feel that this was no ordinary air raid and that we had never experienced anything like it before. And, as it turned out later, we were right for this was our first experience of the *Luftwaffe*[1] which, with great ferocity, attacked the aircraft carrier HMS *Illustrious* as it steamed into the Grand Harbour on her way to the Dockyard for repairs after repeated attacks during her voyage had caused considerable damage. In spite of repeated attacks as she lay at anchor, the carrier managed to survive the ordeal but the devastation caused to the Three Cities, particularly L-Isla, could scarcely be imagined.

At the time from our shelter in Gudja, we could not know what was going on in the harbour except that the raid was exceptionally long and the most ferocious we had experienced so far. The details were soon to be made clear. A couple of hours after the All Clear had sounded my granduncle, Wenzu, who lived with us came home and gave us the news. He was a pensioner from the Royal Navy, a widower without children of his own, who had, twenty five years before, seen action in the Battle of Jutland[2] when the ship he was on was sunk. Uncle Wenz, as we fondly called him, was a great animal lover and to his great sorrow had had to leave behind him at Birgu ten cats which he went to feed every day of the week.

On that fateful Thursday he had walked for that purpose to Birgu as usual. In those days the number of rock-cut shelters was few and, as was his wont, on hearing the air raid warning he took shelter inside St Lawrence's church. When he realized that the raid was taking longer and the rain of bombs was getting heavier he decided to leave the church and hurried to the Fosse where the rock cut shelters provided more security. That decision saved his life. He had barely reached the shelters when a direct hit on the church vestry reduced the building to a mound of rubble burying under it a large number of people who had, like my uncle, sought shelter there. Not one of them lived to tell the tale.[3] He sobbed like a child as he was telling us all this, and now and then broke down. I remember myself breaking down too and weeping uncontrollably as I heard the story of death and destruction that had been visited upon the town.

I had more than enough reason to weep for that attack was a portent of the calamitous times that lay ahead – times of terror, despair, starvation and hardship, times that we who have lived through them can never forget. That first German air raid was soon to be followed by others at short intervals, for day after day and night after night. In fine or stormy weather, Sundays or working days the siren gave warning after warning of impending attacks by airborne machines of destruction. On

Life in rock-hewn homes in the bastions brought families close together with the children giving a helping hand in the daily chores.

Left to right: the author, together with his brothers Mario and Josie, during the war at St. Paul's Bay near the Sirens waterpolo pitch.

A group of children crowding round a woman cooking on an open fire amidst the rubble.

Heating a clothes iron on a *kenur*.

Child wearing a gas mask.

Prayers for an allied victory.

Plaque with names of people from Gudja killed by enemy action.

44

Searching amid the rubble of bombed houses.

Water was provided from open taps at street corners.

Opposite page, top: Carrying water home – which was a frequent daily exercise, and (*bottom*), selling nougat made from the juice of the carob bean.

47

Queuing outside Milk Marketing Undertaking shops and outside the Victory Kitchen were daily chores.

such occasions everyone would lay down any work in hand and seek the nearest shelter. Mothers would pick up their children and carry them to safety while the older folk would hastily grab their bag with their valuables and get someone to help them down into the shelters. In a matter of seconds the streets would be deserted, everyone scurrying underground like mice which have been suddenly disturbed.

Those readers who have never ventured inside an air raid shelter can hardly imagine what it was like to spend hours in such a place. One walked through the entrance and down a flight of some twenty steps cut in the rock; after taking a turn to left or right, another short flight of steps would lead to the main shelter. It was common practice to have the entrance twisting and turning to absorb some of the tremendous blast when a bomb exploded; in that way those sheltering inside would be spared from the effect of the blast. Total darkness reigned inside the shelter, only dimly relieved by the feeble light of a few oil lamps; how similar all this must have been to the atmosphere in the catacombs where our ancient forebears sought safety during the persecutions in the early years of Christianity! The mouldy smell of the damp rock was sickening; the wet rock was freezing to the touch and water would be dripping from the ceiling. On hearing the first rising and falling tones of the siren, people would scuttle to these underground places and the shelters would soon be packed with humanity. The first persons to get inside would find something to sit on but those arriving later would have to remain standing through the duration of the raid. Usually someone in the crowd would begin to recite the rosary and the others would join in; the fervour with which those present participated in the prayers manifested their faith. When the bombing moved closer and explosions began to shake the ground on which they stood the people prayed harder. At the conclusion of the rosary a number of prayers

49

would follow, repeated several times over, like *Sanctus Deus, Sanctus Fortis, Sanctus Immortalis ... Miserere Nobis.* There was a special prayer in Maltese.

> *Qalb ta' Ġesu u ta' Marija*
> *Itfgħu l-bombi fil-baħar jew fil-ħamrija.*

which, translated, ran something like:

> Heart of Jesus, Heart of Mary,
> Make bombs fall in the sea or in the fields.

Prayers over,[4] people would then try to while away the time chatting until some close explosion would make them recite a few more prayers.

As one would expect, there were different sorts of individuals; there were those who were terrified and would shake like a leaf, others less so. Then there were the ones who wanted to appear fearless and therefore tried to show no emotion. I remember some persons who would turn speechless as bombs went off while others would weep. One young woman, I remember, used to throw one hysterical fit after another and at each explosion she would wave her arms about and leap around as if out of her senses. You can imagine what this kind of behaviour would do to the morale of those around! As children we were lucky not to have too much imagination and this helped to shelter us from realizing the true horrors of war. I am told that there were instances of people being literally terrified to death or taking leave of their senses.

Daylight air raids were not as bad as those during the night. You would be sleeping in a warm bed when you were woken up by a voice shouting: "Get out of bed! There's an air raid!" Whether you liked or not, you had to hop out of bed, and quickly at that! We children each had a small straw mattress on which we slept at home; as soon as we were woken up we would take up the mattress and carry it down to the shelter and, once there, we would continue our sleep till the morning. My elder brother, Josie, a sound sleeper if ever there was one, was once woken up in this manner and halfway to the shelter laid his mattress in the middle of the street and lay down to continue his slumbers. In our hurry to get to the shelter, none of us realized that and it had to be one of our neighbours to tell us where he was before any harm came his way.

Living in an air raid shelter was hardship enough: the cold, the damp, the smells, the crowding. But of course that was not the whole story. We struck up good relations with the people of Gudja and some friendships formed during the war years are still strong. But I have a nagging suspicion in my mind that during night raids when, besides women and children, the menfolk used also to go down in the shelters (during the day they would be away from their homes) and therefore the place would be more crowded, some of the villagers would feel that we refugees from the towns were taking their rightful place. It was probably for that reason that clashes sometimes broke out. I remember one occasion when my father got into a heated argument with one of the villagers and I was so scared that I ran out of the shelter and sat on a doorstep with an air raid raging around.

For the sake of truth I have to confess that there were several occasions when during a daylight air raid I did not get into a shelter. My mother regularly made a roll call when the family went into the shelter to make sure that we were all present. My brother Josie and I soon got used to mother's routine check and soon learnt how to get round it: we would simply be there when she called our names and as soon as that was done we would slink out of the shelter so that we could watch the dogfights between "our" planes and "theirs" in the open skies above. Our fighters would chase the enemy aircraft off; these would go through all sorts of manoeuvres to escape

51

and sometimes turn on their attackers, machine guns firing in bursts. The aircraft would turn, twist, dive, shoot up and dive again and now and again one of them would burst into flames and leave a trail of black smoke as it fell to earth. When the stricken plane was one of ours onlookers would fall silent but if it happened to be an Italian or German one, cheering would break out as we looked in expectation to see how the pilot would fare. More often than not the pilot (and other members of the crew if the plane was a bomber) would bale out and float by parachute. Woe betide him if the man happened to be on the enemy side and came down in an inhabited spot! I remember one such incident when a German pilot came down in a nearby field. The word soon went round and on touching the ground he found himself surrounded by a furious crowd, mostly young men and boys: a few farmers ran towards the spot, brandishing their impliments as they ran. The pilot was a fair-headed young man wearing blue overalls. He soon became the target of stone throwing and he was lucky that a detachment of British soldiers arrived in time to take him prisoner and save him from an end more horrible than if he had been killed in his machine.

Occasionally we used to walk to the anti-aircraft battery situated in the fields behind the parish church so that we could watch the gunners manning the *Bofors* in action. To us it was like watching a game of football rather than a struggle for survival, with death ever round the corner. While we were enjoying every moment in this way, mother was in the shelter thinking that my brother and I were somewhere in the same place. As they say, you never know what children can get up to especially when people are living through abnormal and difficult times. People seemed to have fallen into a state of indifference and neglect with the inevitable result that discipline within the family was the first casualty. The very fact that we children could manage to sneak out of the shelter without much difficulty shows that the people were no longer as terrified of the bombardment as they were at the outset of war; people seemed to have become used to air raids even though these, with the advent of the *Luftwaffe*, had become much fiercer as time passed. So much so, that many people could not be bothered to go to shelters in spite of air raid warnings and instead stayed at home, busying themselves with the housework. It is no wonder, therefore, that many lost their lives under the rubble of bombed houses, tragedies that could easily have been avoided if normal precautions had been observed especially when enough shelters were being provided.

Compared to other parts of the Island such as Luqa and the area around the Grand Harbour, Gudja did not suffer as much war damage but it also had its dark hours with the worst disaster striking in April 1942, probably the worst month of the whole war when it seemed as if the German air force was determined to eliminate the Island defences once and for all.[5] That month came to be known as "Black April". Some days before the Gudja tragedy a whole family was wiped out when the small private shelter attached to their home in Tarxien received a direct hit. The headmistress at the Gudja primary school, who lived in Raħal Ġdid and knew the family, advised Karmena, one of the porters at the school , that her family should immediately stop using the private shelter which they had in the yard. Karmena was not impressed at all and smiled as she said, "Do you think that because something like that happened in Tarxien, the story is going to repeat itself here in Gudja?" The headmistress' words turned out to be prophetic. A few days later, on the April 9, a Thursday, at about two in the afternoon, the siren sounded warning. Almost immediately we could hear the din of explosions which sounded quite near. Here I must make an observation: when we left Birgu to avoid the bombardment which was expected to be heaviest in the dockyard area and settled in Gudja we were, in a way, getting out of the frying pan and into the fire, for Gudja lay quite close to the aerodrome at Luqa, one of the prime targets of the German *Luftwaffe*. On that fateful April day we could tell from inside the shelter that the explosions were getting nearer and nearer as the ground under our feet shuddered with every new explosion. The women began to recite one prayer after another but there was no sign of any relaxation of the bombing; if anything it seemed to be getting heavier so that we felt the shelter shake as never before. You could see terror on every face. People huddled together, children grabbed mothers or elder brothers and sisters. The parish priest, Father Anton Rapa, who happened to be in the shelter with us, told us to recite the Act of Contrition and then imparted Absolution. If not for us, for a number of others the end was imminent. After some two hours of continuous bombing the siren signalled the All Clear: the enemy aircraft were returning to their base and that the worst was over. At least that is what everyone in the shelter took to be the case. A certain Zarenu rushed out of the shelter and ran to the house where his mother and sisters lived to check that they were all safe after that raid. On arriving at the alley where the house was situated he saw that the few houses in the alley were reduced to mounds of rubble under which members of his family, including Karmena the school porter, were now buried. Was the conversation which Karmena had had with the headteacher a few days before triggered off with some kind of premonition? Or was it simply a coincidence?

I can still see in my mind's eye the stretchers with the dead covered in blankets being carried down the street where the smell of burnt cordite was still overpowering. In the village the incident not only provoked sorrow for the dead but struck terror among the living. In spite of having taken shelter, a whole family had been wiped out in a matter of seconds. But, as they say, "Time is the great healer" and in a matter of days life returned to normal and certain people soon forgot their fears and began once more to keep away from shelters, staying at home or standing in the middle of the street to watch the dogfights in the skies above them.

No one could however ignore the perils we lived through in those dark years for when life appeared to return to normality there would be some incident which would bring back the realities of a country in a state of siege, with all the perils that implied. That is precisely the experience I went through when I lost a dear friend, the son of Gerit who was a widow. He was the apple of her eye and I think he was somewhat pampered partly because he was the youngest in the family and partly because he had lost his father at a tender age. He was always very attached to his mother, generally hanging on to her apron strings while Gerit, on her part, would never let him out of her sight. One day while with his mother working in the field he found what he took to be a thermos flask half buried in the soil. He took the flask home and with a boy's curiosity decided to find out what was inside the container. He reached for a hammer and struck the top; in all probability the first blow was all that was needed to set the explosive off and in that split second Gerit lost her son, torn to shreds by that bomb. There were many similar incidents like this, especially among young boys.

Pietru, more popularly known as "Bones", used to live on his own in a couple of rooms down the alley near us; as his nickname immediately suggests, he was very thin and emaciated. Summer or winter Pietru never varied his mode of dress: a flannel vest, trousers reaching halfway between knees and ankles, a cap, a clay pipe between his lips, a small sack over his shoulder and feet unencumbered by shoes or sandals. I knew him as a man of few words and as a quiet person. It was common knowledge in the village that Pietru never saw the inside of an air raid shelter in spite of the fact that neighbours used to appeal to him to take shelter during bombing raids and to be more concerned about his safety. When listening to such appeals, he would not say a word but keep on drawing on his pipe but when the tragedy that killed off Karmena and her family struck, Pietru appeared to understand that the appeals were reasonable and ones that should be taken up. Karmena was his next door neighbour and perhaps that was the point that persuaded him to change his ways and to take shelter, especially when the bombing was heavy. A few days after Karmena's death there was a heavy attack and the now converted Pietru dutifully made his way to the shelter. On this occasion, unluckily for him, he did not actually go down but stayed at the entrance and when a bomb hit the entrance and exploded Pietru was killed on the spot. Such incidents seem to lend support to those who believe in destiny.

There were others who unlike Pietru seemed to be destined to come through such experiences unscathed, no matter how close they may have been to death. An instance of what I am saying comes to mind. My aunt (on my father's side) had three children whom she brought up single-handed as her husband, being a Royal Navy man was on duty abroad almost for the duration of the war. One day one of the children, the middle one, was running a high temperature and my aunt was in a state of utter panic, uncertain as to what she would do. When she saw that her son was in that state she decided to stay indoors during the air raid instead of going down to the shelter; as she looked into the street a passer-by was heard saying that a massive attack was on the way with hundreds of bombers approaching the Island. On hearing this, my aunt realized that she had no alternative but to wrap up the child in blankets and seek shelter. The heavy attack, however, did not materialize and only a few sporadic explosions could be heard in the distance. My aunt immediately found an explanation:

the passer-by was either misinformed or he had made up the story to scare people, and she regretted having taken his advice, thereby endangering her son's condition. When the Raiders Passed signal was given and she made her way back to the house, she was dumbstruck to see that the roof of one room had caved in and the heavy stones had smashed the bed in which her son had been lying less than an hour before. Her hour, and that of her son's had not yet come.

One of the most heroic deeds of the war showed the lengths to which a father would go for love of his son. The incident which I am about to recount took place in Gudja; the hero was "is-Sur Tonin" (Borg), a sturdy man standing some six feet in his socks. "Is-Sur Tonin" was a widower with two sons, George the elder and Gawdenz and it was with the elder of the two that one day he went for a ride in his pony trap. When the two arrived at Marsa there was an air raid but since there appeared to be no shelters in the vicinity or, perhaps, because the father thought it was a false alarm, they continued on their way regardless. The raid was heavy and long drawn and at one point the terrified father realized that a few of the bombs released by one of the aircraft were falling in their direction. In an instant the son jumped off the cart and threw himself flat on the ground, as he had been taught to do in similar circumstances. The father, seeing in a flash the imminent danger, instinctively threw himself on his son making himself a human shield. One bomb exploded a few yards away from them making a terrific din. George was unharmed but felt the force of the blast and kept his head down and when things quietened down he slowly raised his head and looked around. He could not believe his eyes. His father was lying dead beside him, his massive body shrunk with the blast. "Is-Sur Nin" had laid down his life for his son. I remember that the father's corpse was removed to Bugeja Hospital[6] at St Venera from where it was to be taken to Gudja for interment in the village cemetery. As was the custom in those days the parish priest asked for two altar boys to volunteer to accompany the funeral party from the hospital to the cemetery. It was thus that my brother and I found ourselves accompanying "is-Sur Tonin" on his last journey. I remember that on the way we had to stop several times because of the frequent air raid warnings with the result that the trip took several hours to complete. The two Birgu kids had done their duty in the hour of need.

Of all the altar boys, my brother and I were the most active and we rarely let a church function go by without in some way or other assisting at it. There would be Mass every day, on Thursdays we had the *Ora Santa* (the Holy Hour), on Sundays there would be a High Mass, catechism classes, benedictions … We took part in the singing whenever the occasion arose and I imagine few of those who heard our performance were transported with delight! But anyhow, we did our best. In a way we were lucky that there was no television at the time and so our singing could not be judged by comparison with that of the professionals. There was in addition to the normal church functions other occasions, the most memorable of which was the Christmas sermon which is traditionally given by a boy. I learned that I would be given that responsibility in September 1941 at the time another brother was born. During the ceremony of baptism the parish priest got in touch with my uncle and asked whether he would agree to my being given the task of delivering the Christmas sermon. My uncle agreed at once and a couple of days later he produced an exercise book with the sermon hand written in ink and told me that he would be teaching it to me page by page. I cannot say that I was brimming with enthusiasm at the idea. My hesitation in taking up the challenge was not due to shyness or anything like that; it was rather that I felt that at my age – I was not yet ten – the responsibility was too heavy for my young shoulders. But the die was cast and there was no more to be said about it: the parish priest had spoken and that was final. So it came about that every morning, before setting off to work, my uncle would sit there and with great patience teach me the sermon, paragraph after paragraph. I sensed that this early morning chore was not a pleasant one for my poor uncle; I proved to be a rather difficult student. He showed his regret at having taken up the parish priest's suggestion more than once and I remember him saying, "If only I knew what I was getting in for! I should never have agreed to the idea." Still, in spite of everything, I managed to learn the whole sermon in good time. When the day came, and I delivered the sermon without a hitch, my relatives, especially my grandmother were inordinately proud of me and, as for myself, I enjoyed immensely the popularity which the Christmas sermon bestows on the boy who delivers it.

In that year the "midnight" Mass was celebrated in a packed church at four in the afternoon. As I stepped down from the pulpit at the conclusion of my sermon I overheard an oldish woman ask another, "Whose son is he? Isn't he clever?" (I do not think that I was any better than other boys who had done this sermon before me.) The other woman replied, "He's not from these parts. He belongs to the refugees who live in the MUSEUM building." I doubt that any priest from Birgu had ever preached the Saint Mary panegyric in the Gudja church. If that is so then one may safely say that the tradition was kept alive by a ten year old boy on that particular Christmas which fell in the fiercest part of the war.

The reader might here wonder, "What would happen if an air raid warning was sounded in the middle of a religious function?" To the best of my knowledge, and here my memory might be letting me down, most of the congregation would probably go on with their prayers because they firmly believed that being inside a church, especially during prayers, was as safe as being in a shelter; their faith was boundless. On the other hand there were those whose fear was stronger than their faith and these would rush to the nearest shelter at the first sign of an attack. As for us altar boys, we used to go on with whatever we were engaged in at that moment. But there were exceptions to that rule: in my case I sometimes left my post for the safety of the shelter. One instance I remember clearly was when I was serving at a requiem Mass at about six in the morning. I was in charge of the censer that day and I was behind the altar fanning the embers in the censer when there was an air raid warning. None of us appeared to take the least notice until we realized that the explosions were getting nearer and that the enemy bombers would soon be overhead. An instant later there was an ear-splitting explosion, a shower of shattered glass fell around us and the whole church shuddered. As a boy I had a lively imagination and after the first shock was over I felt scared that the church would collapse on us all. In the terrified state I was in I hurled the censer with the burning embers in it away from me and dashed to the nearest shelter which was in the church square. I can still picture in my mind the puzzled look on the faces of those in the shelter when they saw this miniature priest who was me scurrying with all his might to safety. The raid was soon over and when I went back the other boys started kidding me and I am sure that I would never have qualified for a medal for bravery! Perhaps they were right. But on the other hand I could not be blamed for deserting my post for the safety of a shelter. After all, why should I risk my life during a mass for the dead?

At about that time, that is the spring of 1942, over and above the fear of air raids another fear began to gain ground: the fear of an invasion.[7] As children, we could never grasp the full import of but could understand that we would be subjected to a heavy bombardment after which paratroops would drop on us from every quarter. To me the idea of seeing German soldiers in our streets was like an obsessive nightmare and I remember myself trying to figure out how long we would be able to stay in our air raid shelters before we had to go out. I seem to vaguely remember the issuing of instructions by the authorities as to what people should do in the event of an invasion.

Strange as it may seem, it was an exercise to simulate an invasion that, to a certain extent, calmed my fears. Among those taking part in the exercise were members of the Home Guard recruited from among those men who for one reason or another (as, for example, age or employment) had not been conscripted into the regular army but who were still considered capable of carrying arms in an emergency. During this exercise the people were ordered to stay indoors. We went to our rooftop to watch proceedings and wondered when we saw men hiding behind rubble walls, pointing their shotguns at others who in turn raised their arms above their heads in exactly the same way as we often saw in films. Those taking part in the exercise naturally used blank ammunition with the exception of a certain Karmnu. One cannot tell for certain whether it was because Karmnu had not used his gun for some considerable time or perhaps because he wanted to put some realism into the exercise; the fact remains that he had live ammunition in his old gun and when he drew the trigger he shot one of his companions in the arm. The victim demanded satisfaction and the incident looked as if it would take a serious turn and end up with having two casualties. We wondered what would happen if a real invasion took place when a simple exercise was already leaving casualties. I have always thought that the Germans were lucky not to proceed with the planned invasion. Karmnu ended up being the butt of not very complimentary comments. After that exercise, which resembled a game rather than real warfare, I seem to have shed at least part of my fears of the invasion.

Notes and references

1. The first *Luftwaffe* attack took place on January 16, 1941 when some thirty two bombers of the type *Junker 88* targeted HMS *Illustrious*, HMS *Perth* and the mv *Breconshire*. The attack began at 1.50 p.m. The German planes dived very steeply and terrified the population with their new style of attack. No one could deny their fearless determination. The incessant attack lasted some two hours during which tremendous damage was caused. In l-Isla alone hundreds of homes were razed to the ground. Hundreds of other houses were demolished in Birgu and Bormla while in Old Mint Street, Valletta a number of common tenement houses were reduced to rubble when a stricken plane crashed into the locality. The merchant-man *Essex* which happened to be unloading the cargo in the Grand Harbour received two direct hits. In this attack alone 57 civilians were killed mainly in Birgu and l-Isla, while another 29 suffered serious injuries. All enemy planes which were hit came down in the sea and not a single airman survived. Immediately following this terrifying attack, Valletta, Birgu, Bormla and l-Isla were evacuated once again.

2. The battle of Jutland was fought on May 31, 1916. The British Fleet under Admiral Sir John Jellicoe engaged the German fleet under the command of Admiral Reinhard Scheer in one of the greatest naval battles in history. Several Maltese and Gozitan seamen lost their lives serving on the battleship HMS *Queen Mary*, the cruisers HMS *Black Prince* and HMS *Defence*, the destroyer HMS *Shark* and other units. (V Wickman)

3. At least 30 people are known to have perished in the vestry of the church of St Lawrence when they sought shelter during the attack. Several artistic treasures held in the church were badly damaged or destroyed outright.

4. There were various prayers specially written or composed which people recited during air raids. One such prayer implored Our Lady's intercession:

Reġina tal-Vittorji,	Queen of victories,
Reġina tas-Sema w l-Art,	Queen of Heaven and Earth,
Ilqa' l-bombi fil-mant tieghek	Gather the bombs in Thy mantle
U ehlisna minn dan l-attakk.	And deliver us from this attack.

Another written in English was a prayer for gunners, pilots, wardens and firemen:

Bless this shelter, Lord, we pray,
During air raids night and day:
Bless the people here within,
Keep them safe and free from sin.
>Bless the gunners as they work,
>The searchlight guide when dangers lurk:
>Bless each chasing aircraft crew,
>Lend Thine aid to all they do.
Bless the members of Thy flock,
Keep them free from air raid shock;
Bless the light and keep it bright,
And away from alien light.
>Bless our wardens one and all,
>Answering their country's call;
>Our gallant firemen, help them Lord,
>Let Thy grace be their reward.
Bless all those who work for peace
That hostilities may cease.

(Philip Vella, *Malta Blitzed but not Beaten*)

5. April 1942: Some 6000 tons of bombs were dropped on Malta in the
course of this month. Civilian deaths were in the region of 300 while
hundreds of others were badly injured. At the end of the month it was
officially claimed that 101 enemy planes had been destroyed by anti-
aircraft batteries and 54 were brought down by RAF fighters. By the end
of 1942 it was estimated that over 14,000 tons of bombs were dropped
on the island, the equivalent of about 100 tons over every square mile.
During the war the number of air raid alerts was 3215. Civilian deaths
amounted to 1468 which in a population of around 270,000 gives a rate
of one person in every 200. Enemy losses amounted to 1129 planes
as against Allied losses of 568. (*The Air Battle of Malta, 1945*). Some
40,000 buildings – houses, schools, churches – were destroyed or badly
damaged. (C.J. Boffa)

6. Bugeja Hospital (now Ċentru Ħidma Soċjali, Sta Venera) was opened in
the first weeks after June 11, 1940. It was one of the emergency hospitals
which had been prepared by the authorities to cope with the heavy
casualties which were expected to result from the air bombardment (C.J.
Boffa). Fortunately casualties were much lighter probably due to the
fact that the *Luftwaffe* did not strike earlier and by the time it did, rock-
cut shelters were available to the whole population. If the Germans had

started the blitz at the time the Italians carried out their ineffective raids, the casualty rate would have been much higher and the authorities' apprehensions would have been thoroughly vindicated.

7. The Italians expected to take Malta without a struggle when Mussolini declared war on Britain and France in June 1940 following the armistice with France. But Britain continued the struggle and Malta stood up to the haphazard bombing of the Italian air force. The island stood astride the convoy routes between Italy and Libya and warships, submarines, and aircraft from Malta took a heavy toll of the Axis supply ships so that in December 1941 Hitler ordered the Luftwaffe to mount an all-out second air offensive against the Island and the Italians started planning an assault codenamed C3/Herkules to included landings by Italian and German paratroop regiments. But Hitler was highly apprehensive of the losses which would be incurred, citing the heavy losses of the German parachutists in the assault on Crete in May 1941; he also distrusted the Italians. The target date was to be mid-July 1942 but the successes of the German Afrika Korps in advancing to the Egyptian frontier led to the postponement of the original plans as this seemed to make an attack on Malta unnecessary. But the British forces counter-attacked in October 1942 and eventually drove the Axis forces from Libya and, in the end, from North Africa. Sicily was invaded by British and American forces assembled east and west of Malta on July 10, 1943 and the Italian fleet surrendered at Malta two months later, on September 8. Although the enemy forces earmarked for C3/Herkules vastly outnumbered the defenders, various Italian generals thought an attack on the Island would have been *un disastro senza nome* (an unmitigated disaster).

CHAPTER 6

Games and pastimes

At this point readers may find themselves under the impression that "war children" like me did not have a normal childhood. That impression does not correspond to the reality at all for, in spite of what was going on around us, we never forgot that we were children and in the intervals between one air raid and another our behaviour was very similar to what one would expect from children of my age: running around and playing games as if there was no war at all. However, I must say that as far as ordinary toys were concerned we simply did not have any; in fact I do not recollect having at the time as much as a cloth ball to kick around. We had therefore, willy-nilly, to play soldiers. It was a common sight to see boys of my age walking around with a couple of empty corned beef tins slung on our hips in imitation of the ammunition packs carried by soldiers and a stick on our shoulder to make do as a rifle. Equipped like that, we would spend hours having drill parades as our leader shouted at the top of his voice:

Stand-at-Ease!	*Slope Arms!*
Atten-tion!	*Quick March!*
Pre-sent Arms!	*Dis-miss!*

Such were the commands that we heard every day as we stood in admiration watching real soldiers at their training. For the soldiers, of course, it was not much of an entertainment. Perhaps one of the most characteristic traits of the British race is that they can see the funny side of even the most serious matter. The Maltese, I think, were quick to imitate the British in this aspect and throughout the duration of the war numerous songs, mostly doggerel, were improvised to be sung to popular tunes. Perhaps the most popular were those sung to the German tune of *Lilli Marlene*, which had also become a favourite with British troops. One version in Maltese went like this:

> *Hemm trid tarana għaddejjin,*
> *Wara xulxin…*
> *Nhar ta’ Ħamis…*
> *Aħfrilhom, O Sinjur!*

which can be roughly translated as

> You should see us marching along,
> In tight formation,
> Every Thursday,
> Forgive them , Oh Lord!.

Another favourite, this time sung to an English tune, *She'll be coming round the mountain*, ran as follows:

> *Kelli dgħajsa illi biha kont nistad,*
> *Ġiet il-lieva u ġabruni għal suldat*
> *Minn sinjur ġabuni fqir*
> *Kelli nuża l-azzarin*
> *Singing ay, ay, Yuppee, Yuppee, ay.*

> *Kont qed nilbes il-piġama daqq air raid,*
> *Jien tlajt niġri sitta sitta fuq il-bejt*
> *Dawwart wiċċi ma nafx x'rajt*
> *Rajt id-dija tas-searchlight*
> *Singing ay, ay, Yuppee, Yuppee, ay.*

which can be roughly translated as

> I had a boat which I used for fishing,
> Came conscription and I was recruited,
> I was a rich man, reduced now to begging,
> I had to carry a rifle,
> Singing ay, ay, Yuppee, Yuppie, ay.

> As I was getting into my pyjamas,
> there was an air raid warning,
> I bounded upstairs to the rooftop,
> I'm not sure what I was looking at,
> I saw the glare of the searchlight beam,
> Singing ay, ay, Yuppie Yuppie, ay.

Naturally most, but not all, of the songs were based on the military life and routine, The following is another typical song which though having as its subject a man from the Services, has a romantic theme running through it. It tells of a sailor or soldier singing a farewell song to his beloved:

O Katie, Katie sejjer insiefer,	Oh Katie, my Katie, I'm leaving this land,
O Katie, Katie sejjer immur	Oh Katie, Katie, I'm off
Bis-sorra f'idi,	Kitbag in my hand,
Bid-dmugħ f'għajnejja,	With tears in my eyes,
Ejja wassalni sa ħdejn il-vapur!	Come to see me off!
Is-searchlight tefa' fuq id-destroyer	The searchlight lights up the destroyer
Il-bastimenti kollha ħerġin,	The fleet sails out,
O Katie, Katie	Oh Katie, dear Katie,
Nerġgħu niltaqgħu,	We'll meet again,
Jekk Mussolini jħallina ħajjin!	If Mussolini doesn't kill us!

We sang and played a lot then. We had quite a few other games besides playing at soldiers. I need hardly say that in those days, with the exception of one at Floriana, there were no children's playgrounds with swings and slides. But there was a substitute! Access to shelters was down a flight of steps over which was laid a sloping concrete roof; this provided an excellent slide down which we would slide over and over again. Someone in authority, however, apparently did not like to see boys enjoying themselves in this fashion for later on the roof of the stairway was made in such a way – by means of a number of protuberances – that using it as a slide became impossible. What a pity that in such adverse circumstances boys could not indulge in such a simple pastime!

Another favourite game was *il-ħarba*, which consisted of children running away and hiding to avoid being caught by *il-qattus* (the cat). Naturally one of the most convenient hiding places was the shelter, every nook and cranny of which we knew in spite of it being in total darkness. *Il-qattus* certainly did not have an easy job to perform!

Surrounded by open countryside, the village of Gudja was the ideal place for spending long hours roaming around in the fields and country lanes. I can still feel a thrill when I remember the day I went bird-trapping with a friend and his father. Even now, when I have grown to disapprove bird-trapping, I can still recall the intense pleasure of seeing the net fold over to trap the birds under it. I have the same feeling when I remember the days we used to go trapping robins – a pastime which now I would like to see the end of. I also remember the day I was invited to go bird-hunting with a friend and his grandfather and the latter managed to bring down a hawk.

The threshing floor was another source of enjoyment; I remember, as if it was only yesterday, the somersaults and rolling about in the straw, on clear summer nights, which provided me with as much pleasure as can be got these days from swings, slides and similar apparatus in children's playgrounds. I used to envy the village children running around barefoot on the twigs left over after the harvesting of the clover when, as for myself, I could scarcely manage to do so with my shoes on. Later on, of course, I got used to going barefoot and by the time we had to leave the village I could run barefoot with the best of the local children on any sort of terrain.

Another pastime which we had, and which thankfully has disappeared, was trying to bring down swallows with long reeds. With the advent of summer large numbers of swallows would fill the village square, diving down as if in imitation of the German dive bombers to which we had become so accustomed. The swallows would skim the ground and then rise up with great speed. Waving long reeds we would try to knock the swallows down with, I am happy to report, very limited success.

One particular craze in those days was for obtaining objects made from mica, the material then used for cockpit windows in aircraft instead of glass. Once you got hold of a piece of mica you could produce various objects: small crucifixes, rings, butterflies and so on. Probably the most popular of these were the rings. The raw material, mica, could only be obtained from the wreckage of downed RAF and enemy aircraft and crowds of boys would gather around the wrecked plane to try to obtain pieces of aluminium, canvas and, of course, as being most in demand, mica.

The "mica craze" almost cost me my life. With my brother Josie and Ġużi – the first boy I made friends with in Gudja – I was much taken up with producing mica rings which we sold for a penny or a penny-halfpenny apiece. We made brisk business and lots of children, mostly girls, came from every corner of the village to buy our wares and sales flourished until one day we ran out of raw material and the business ground to a halt. The immediate problem was how to get the mica. Airplanes did not just crash on your doorstep when you needed them! My brother and Ġużi had a sudden inspiration:

why not go to Karwija where the RAF kept some fighters in pens? We would certainly be able to sneak into one of the pens and smash a cockpit window and carry the mica home. Putting words into action, we got hold of a couple of light tools and set off towards Karwija.

When we reached the place there seemed to be no guards around and we had no difficulty in getting into one of the pens and scrambling up on one of the plane wings, we began to smash one of the windows. To this day I cannot understand how during a war planes could be left unattended in this way, making sabotage an easy matter. While engaged in our work I shouted that I could hear the siren signalling an air-raid. My brother and Gużi, a couple of boys who were not easily scared and did not like any interruptions in the job in hand, pretended not to hear the siren and my brother told me to shut up. "I told you not to come with us! Why didn't you stay at home?", he screamed at me. I was now doubly terrified: an air raid was imminent and my brother was furious at me. I found the courage to mumble and answer: "Alright, I didn't hear anything! We can finish the job now." At this, my brother seemed to feel that he was responsible for our safety and said that now that I had spoilt the day's work we had to leave immediately. We slid off the wing and threw ourselves flat on the ground behind a rubble wall. It was not a moment too soon! The anti-aircraft battery in the vicinity opened up and before you could blink an eyelid we were in the centre of a battle. At one point we heard a whistling sound and the plane we had been "working on" was a mass of flames, struck by a direct hit. We were speechless with terror especially when we realized that we had escaped a horrible fate by the skin of our teeth. I could not help patting myself on the back seeing that it was my being scared that had saved the lives of the three of us.

CHAPTER 7

School life during the war

When my family left Birgu for Gudja I had been attending Standard I in the Primary School and when we took up residence as refugees in that village I found myself promoted to Standard II without having to go through the annual examination. The class I was placed in occupied one of the rooms in the parish priest's house. Schools, clubs and other public buildings had been requisitioned to house the large number of refugees and therefore classes had to be accommodated elsewhere, as for example, in chapels, churches or in the residence of some person who could afford to provide a room where lessons could be given; in my case, as I have said, it was the parish priest who offered one of the rooms in his house to the Education Department.[1] I remember as if it was only yesterday, our teacher doing her best to see that our education went on normally even though we were in the throes of war; that teacher, Miss Spiteri, I regret to say, was to die in the prime of life. For us children the happiest moments were when the siren sounded an air raid and we would rush out of the class to scurry down into a nearby shelter. For the teacher, of course, such moments occurring midway through a lesson must have been very frustrating indeed. At times our stay in the shelter would be for a few minutes, at other times for much longer as for instance a whole morning. A schoolboy's life in those days was far different from what it is today: we did not have free exercise books or free milk then, no educational visits, no school television or radio programmes, no games. In those days we would not even dream of such things.

I was indeed lucky in my two years of schooling in Gudja to have two excellent teachers. My teacher in Standard Three, Miss Farrugia, had all the qualities you would wish for in a teacher: for her, teaching was the supreme vocation. She possessed that rare talent of being able to show that she really cared for you and wanted to do all she could for you while at the same time imperceptibly exerting firm control of her class. None of us children – not even the most intractable of us - would ever dare to play the fool during a lesson. The class was a mixed one with the boys sitting in the front rows and the girls in the rear. As one would expect each of the boys had his own favourite among the girls; there was one particular girl, blue eyed and raven haired, who was the dream girl for all the boys. I was one of the brighter pupils in the class and even the girls often copied my work without me raising any objection to the practice. Such behaviour on my part did not go down well with one of my classmates, Ġanni by name, who was like me an altar boy in the parish, and who more than once threatened to report my misdemeanour to the parish priest. I could not imagine how the parish priest could be called in the matter; as far as I know altar boys were not bound under a vote of celibacy!

Miss Farrugia was the sort of teacher who believed that in addition to normal lessons children should also be taught about the world outside the school walls and she kept us informed of the progress of the war in its various theatres; I remember her putting a large map over the blackboard as she showed us the places which were being occupied by the German army in its invasion of Russia. The soldiers, we were told, were kept on the alert every minute of the day and could not find the time to get washed with the inevitable consequence of becoming infested with lice. I was really impressed by that!

Naturally, in those days of deprivation, there was a scarcity of everything not just food: we did not have textbooks, exercise books, pencils or erasers. We used to write even on the cover of the exercise books and we would use even the wide space at the top of each page; writing used to be done in pencil so that we could rub off the work and use the page over and over again. When we did not have any proper paper to write on we would often write on wrapping paper or any other paper that came to hand; I remember using an old invoice book, one instance that comes to my mind.

I cannot help smiling when I recall a particular incident related to my schooldays. It so happened that a few doors down from where we lived there was a very fat woman whose daughter was equally plump. Both mother and daughter were endowed with an exceptionally fine complexion, blue eyes and rosy cheeks, the latter often enhanced or rather exaggerated by the cosmetic means of those days. The woman's husband was employed as a street sweeper in Valletta, to be precise in the old railway tunnel which was then being used as an air raid shelter by a few hundred persons. For some reason or other, possibly because bus services were very erratic, the husband often stayed away from home for weeks on end.

On one particular occasion the man did not turn up at home for a longer period than usual and the wife decided to take some steps to remedy the situation. She approached my mother and asked her to make me write a letter to her husband. I readily agreed to the proposal and duly went to her house armed with pencil and exercise book, prepared to do my best in my first commission as a scribe. I wrote out the address and the date at the top with the appropriate commas and full stops just as the teacher had taught us to do a couple of months or so before. I then started a fresh line: "Dear ..." and waited for the woman to begin her dictation. I was expecting her to start off with the usual rubric, "I am writing these few lines to tell you that thanks to God we are in good health and hope that this letter will find you in the best of health too." What happened next was totally different. "Write!" she said, "*You wretched dog, is this how you treat your wife and your daughter ...*" and then went on in this vein for line after line while I willy-nilly had to put down imprecation after imprecation. When she realized that I was getting more and more uncomfortable, she prodded me on, "Go on, write! ... Wasn't it you who accepted to write the letter for me?" There was nothing for me to do but to take down her words, as she said them, without any attempt to leave out some of the more improper vocabulary. To this day I have no idea as to the effect this letter had on the wayward husband but I can safely say that the letter was not the sort that marriage guidance counsellors would approve of. When I finally finished the letter the poor woman gave me a penny for my pains.

Standard Three was the top class in the school at Gudja and pupils who wanted to move on with their studies beyond that stage had to get a transfer to the Luqa primary school. My brother, Josie, did precisely that and since there was no public transport between the two villages he had to cover the distance on foot day after day. That took him some twenty or thirty minutes each way; when, in the proper season, he had to pass fields which had something to offer, as for instance, beans, the trip would take much longer. At this time air raids were getting heavier and more frequent and my parents decided that my brother could not be allowed to run such risks and therefore it would be better for him to repeat Standard Three at the Gudja school.

As one would expect lessons were not always held regularly. I can now appreciate the dedication and care which our teachers showed during those times of stress and shortages, when we were walking on the edge of a precipice. Teachers then could easily have used the war as an excuse (a justified excuse, I would imagine) for taking their responsibilities lightly. Most teachers took the difficult situation in their stride and would more often than not work harder to make up for time lost during air raids. This, I think, could be said for the majority of teachers. When one realizes that most of our present day leaders received at least part of their education during those hard times one can only express admiration for those dedicated teachers.

Notes and references

1. Education suffered a serious setback during the war. Many schools were closed down or were used to store foodstuffs while others were transformed into refugee centres. The education system, like the judiciary, was thoroughly disturbed. On January 19, 1941 schools were closed down for a couple of weeks and teachers were instructed to report for duty at the Protection Offices.

CHAPTER 8

The return from Gudja

My brother and I had had become thoroughly used to living in Gudja and memories of living in Birgu had begun to fade. In our speech we still had the Cottonera accent, including the characteristic way of pronouncing the letter *Q* but our vocabulary had taken on board new words like *ħada* (near), *bini l-ġuħ/l-għatx* (I'm hungry/thirsty), *waddab* (throw) and so on. We had grown to pronounce the vowels in the Gudja manner whereby the sound *a* is pronounced as *o*. We had become, so to say, part and parcel of the village scene. We had come to know every lane, every alley and every field in and around Gudja. Because of the smallness of the locality we knew the names, the surnames and nicknames of almost every villager and in turn we were known by practically all of them. We had grown to be so fond of the small village that one of my dreams was that my father would be tempted to rent a house and, of course, a field so that we could live in Gudja for the rest of our lives. That dream was not as fantastic as it appears at first sight for although my father, a Dockyard worker, was born and bred in Birgu, a few metres away from the sea, he had, like my brother and myself, grown to like the fields and the simple, rural life as lived in the village. In fact I now feel sure that if we had stayed in Gudja until the end of the war, the temptation to take up residence there would have been irresistible. But that was not to be: what to us children was fun was something totally different to grown-ups who must have felt that their roots were elsewhere.

At this stage in my life I think I can well imagine the sadness which my father and mother and my other relatives must have experienced on leaving their comfortable homes to go and live in cramped quarters in a strange village with customs and usages which were very different from those to which they had been accustomed from childhood. The cramped environment of their new home was probably the worst part of it all: six families living in the narrow confines of a small house, sleeping, eating, washing and cooking in the few rooms and corridor which made up the sum total of the accommodation.

The menfolk, mainly Dockyard workers like my father and my uncle, had another problem besides the bombing and the cramped accommodation: transport to and from the work-place. When the situation took a turn for the worse and petrol became unavailable, transport ground to a halt except for one or two trips a day performed by buses.[1] Dockyard workers had no choice but to walk all the way to the harbour area day in, day out. The daily walk to work was fraught with danger and was some four or five miles each way – certainly not a pleasant walk after a hard day's work. Air raids were common and shelters were not always at hand; where shelters were available these consisted of slit trenches cut in the soil of the fields which bordered the road – never as safe as the rock-cut shelters in the built up areas. The trenches only afforded protection from flying shrapnel – as the iron fragments from exploding bombs were called.

The daily trips to the Dockyard were clearly taking toll of my father's health and the decision was taken to leave Gudja for a place which would be nearer to the workplace. Birgu was out of the question partly because of the frequent bombing around the area and partly because most of the houses, including our former home, were destroyed or severely damaged. The "Big Four" – my father, my mother, my uncle and my aunt – put their heads together and agreed that we should move to Raħal Ġdid, a decision which did not go down well with us children who however could only bow our heads and comply. To us that meant destroying the roots which we had formed in Gudja and moving to a completely alien place. It was now June of 1942 and the worst part of the bombardment was behind us. But two new threats, no less terrible than the bombardment, now appeared on the scene: the food shortages and scabies.

My first experience of the food shortage was when I heard people say that food supplies were running so low that rationing would be coming into effect soon.[2] When it was explained to me that rationing meant that I would not be able to eat as much as I wanted to I received the news with a great deal of trepidation. I had a reputation within the family of being a glutton, certainly an apt description especially if one compared me to Josie who was a delicate child and often refused food. My brother's reluctance in his eating habits was a constant source of worry to my mother. Not so to me! No sooner would I finish off my plate than I would turn to my brother's and finish it off for him. I must say that during our stay in Gudja I never experienced hunger or, for that matter, scabies but I was soon to have a taste of the two after settling in Raħal Ġdid.

The day on which we were to leave Gudja for Raħal Ġdid saw us load our few belongings on a donkey cart hired for the purpose. Our driver, the owner of the ancient grey donkey was a stout young man with blue eyes and a freckled face. It is still for me a matter of amazement how that small cart could have carried so many people in addition to our belongings; my mother, my grandmother and the young children all found a place on that cart. The rest of us, together with my aunt, did the trip on foot. Some of our relatives stayed on at Gudja for some time. It was thus that after two years of adventures and new experiences we left the charming village of Gudja. Those two years were to leave a lasting impression on me: two years during which I could taste the unspoilt village life; two years which taught me the beauty of my mother tongue as spoken and handled by the sons of farmers; two years which imbued me with a fascination for all things Maltese especially that language which not only serves our daily purposes but also provides us with a national identity.

Notes and references

1. Public Transport was also badly hit during the war years. As from July 3, 1940, the sale of petrol for private cars was stopped. Doctors, government engineers and senior health inspectors were entitled to a ration of petrol. Though the sale of petrol was strictly controlled, buses still ran although with very restricted services. On July 14, 1940 private cars were banned from the streets and omnibuses and *karozzini* (both horse-drawn) made a re-appearance in the streets of Malta.

2. The following commodities were rationed: bread, milk, sugar, butter, oil, rice, pasta, paraffin, cigarettes, matches, wool, animal fodder, cement, etc. Things which were not rationed could only be purchased after hours of standing in a queue. Certain commodities were rationed as from April 7, 1941. To make up for the flour shortage the extraction rate at the milling stage was raised from the normal 50 or 60 percent to some 82 percent with the result that the colour of the loaf of bread changed from white to brown due to the increase in the proportion of bran.

A signal post constructed with stones from bombed sites reflected the
games children played.

One way to evade standing in the queue for the kerosene cart was to place the cans in line.

Young girls kept themselves occupied playing with dolls or cooking for the family in the open, while the boys found time to display their patriotism.

A scene of devastation at Paola (Raħal Ġdid), after a heavy night raid in which several persons were killed.

Antonio Borg

George Borg

Cooking - watercolour by Alfred Gerada. *(Courtesy Albert Ganado)*

THE *SANTA MARIJA CONVOY* EN ROUTE TO MALTA. Painting by John Hamilton.
(Imperial War Mueum)

Cheering the arrival of the tanker *Ohio* during Operation Pedestal.

Children posing for a photo round the wreckage of a German bomber.

Cheering the British Prime Minister, Winston Churchill, as he tours the Dockyard, accompanied by the Governor, Lord Gort, and the Admiral Malta, Vice-Admiral Sir Ralph Leatham.

Children celebrating in front of the Paola Information Bureau.

CHAPTER 9

Raħal Ġdid

To this day I am still not quite sure as to who made it first to Raħal Ġdid, whether it was the patient donkey drawing the cart with all our possessions or those of us who went all the way on foot. What I know for certain is that as soon as we arrived at Raħal Ġdid I distinctly sensed that we had stepped into a different world altogether. One is at a loss to explain how in a small place like Malta one can find so many differences between one village and another in the way people live. Such differences have now more or less disappeared mainly due to the effects of the media, such as the Rediffusion network, radio, television and the newspapers and also the widely used transport system by means of which people from the different localities mix at school and at the work-place. In 1942 the situation was totally different. The way of life as lived in a particular village was different from that lived in one of the towns and Raħal Ġdid, in spite of its name (the "New Village" as it is called locally) was a progressive urban community. Raħal Ġdid had made giant strides in terms of population growth in the immediate pre-war decades and at the time of our settling there had become an extensive residential area stretching from the monumental Addolorata Cemetery at one end to Ghajn Dwieli at the other end and from Ta' Lourdes (near Corradino) to the then hamlet of Fgura – an enormous area when compared to the small village of Gudja.

The street we were about to settle in consisted of four large blocks of houses, with each block having some twenty houses so that the street contained about eighty houses. Our house was a typical one: four rooms, a backyard with a few pockets of soil and the overlying rooftop. We now had all the water we needed at the turn of a tap as well as the sanitary facilities such as a proper toilet and a bathroom, which were all missing at Gudja and which now made us feel as if we were entering a paradise on earth. All dreams of paradise however turned out to be short-lived; two of the rooms, we soon discovered, had only half a roof to shelter the inmates from the elements so that from the groundfloor you could see the sun shining from above during the day and the stars twinkling in the night. The matter was soon put right by spanning the open spaces with planks. Every window pane in the house had been shattered by the blast of exploding bombs falling in the vicinity and the electricity supply was cut. As the old folk say, "There's only one thing you cannot do anything about: death", and things soon took a turn for the better.

A few days after our moving into the house the roofs were patched up so that when the first rains fell in September we could keep reasonably dry. The window panes took longer to be replaced and we had to do with makeshift ones as practically everybody had been forced to do; the glass was replaced by coarse white linen. Linen, one need hardly say, is not transparent and did not allow much light into the house but at least it protected us from the cold winds. We also had to wait for a long while before the electricity supply was restored and we had to use paraffin lamps with glass tubes. The light from these lamps was dim compared to the normal light bulbs and there was the added nuisance of having to trim the wick and polish the tube ever so often. Glass tubes were difficult to come by in those days and you had to exercise great care when cleaning them. Even paraffin was scarce and rationed and we had to use it sparingly. Paraffin stoves, the cookers of those days, were often replaced by the traditional wood-burning "kenur" made of stone. But then again firewood for it was in short supply and children spent hours looking for the odd bit of wood, generally among the rubble of bombed out buildings. You could see children of all ages carrying bits of wood, faggots, broken doors and timber beams, anything that burns, to their homes so that mothers could do the cooking.

On our first afternoon at Raħal Ġdid, I went out with my brother to explore the neighbourhood and its inhabitants. Our first encounter with the local children was when we met a few boys of our age sitting on a doorstep; we quickly made friends. It so happened that two of the boys were the sons of a neighbouring family when we lived at Birgu. That first meeting with children who had been used to living in a town instead of, as in my case, a rural district made me aware of how different they were from my friends at Gudja. Our new friends were much tidier and instead of nicknames were known as the son of Mrs X or of Mrs Y. No one was called Konsu, Ġanni, Ġerit, Rożi or Żeppa as was the case in Gudja. The conversation between these new friends tended to be about girls and it appeared to me that all of them had girlfriends. My Gudja mates seemed to be interested exclusively in bird-trapping, kittens and puppies and other topics invariably connected with animals and nature.

Children rarely take a long time to adapt to new circumstances and they tend to make, and forget, friends easily. I soon had a new circle of friends from Raħal Ġdid (although to this day I still count among my friends several hailing from Gudja) and when my first day at Raħal Ġdid was drawing to an end and it was time to go home, I could not help wishing for the coming morrow when I would be able to meet my new friends again.

At about this time air raids had diminished in frequency and intensity so that we often had a string of days without any forays by enemy aircraft. We began to count ourselves lucky that the destruction we had been used to was now becoming a rarity. People now could set their minds at rest since there were shelters in adequate numbers and at this stage of the war several of the shelters even had electricity laid on. It was the sick and the aged that now bore the brunt of the circumstances of the war and who had to be carried down to the dank and cold shelters – the modern version of the catacombs of ancient times – sometimes in the middle of the night. The night air raids, I think, were the hardest to bear when you could be woken up in the early hours, get out of the warm bedding and into the damp shelter; at times this could happen three or more times during one night. Many people, in fact, used to spend the whole night in the shelter without stepping outside before morning.

On our arrival at Raħal Ġdid we saw ruined houses wherever we looked; the constant bombing of the past months had taken its toll, the direct result of its vicinity to the Dockyard and the harbour. Hundreds of buildings were razed to the ground and hundreds of others had gaping holes in the roof, collapsed balconies or badly damaged doors and windows. In the main square itself there was a large crater which had penetrated the huge reservoir when a heavy bomb fell and the blast of the explosion killed a number of people who were taking shelter nearby. One man lost his life when in pitch darkness he stumbled and fell into the reservoir and drowned.

CHAPTER 10

Starvation and scabies

I am still not quite sure as to what causes the condition known as scabies or, as it is called in the vernacular, *il-ħakk* ("the itch"). Probably the vitamin deficiencies, coupled with anxiety and stress caused by the war, had much to do with the condition. Whatever the cause, the fact is that it was a cruel disease. Generally, the first symptoms to appear were tiny pustules or pimples on the skin between the fingers followed by insufferable itching which made you scratch, causing the itching to become even worse. In some cases the pustules were larger and spread all over the body. I remember people who, as a result of the symptoms appearing on the back, could neither sit nor lie on their backs. The standard remedy, if one can call it like that, was to apply a purplish ointment to the skin several times a day. To this day I still have serious doubts about the efficacy of that particular medicine. One statement can be made with certainty: now that the bombing had all but ceased and we could sleep tranquilly during nights, this new condition had to appear and make life hell for many of us. With very few exceptions children caught the itch and you could see around you girls and boys covered with sores from head to toes. I was not too badly struck by the condition but I still had to be medicated regularly and rubbed with the ointment. The itch was not confined to children and adults were just as likely to be affected. Apparently servicemen had to undergo a more drastic treatment as their skin was scratched until it bled and then the sores were allowed to dry up in time.

The itch was certainly a most insidious ailment but not as bad as hunger. In my opinion hunger was even worse than the bombing. I can well believe that those who lost relatives during the war through bombing will take a different view of the situation and I myself would probably share that view in those circumstances. But the reader has to keep in mind that I am writing this narrative of the war as seen through the eyes of a boy; we could with relative ease evade the bombing by going into the shelters but there was no way of running away from hunger. I cannot remember precisely the date when the bread ration was reduced to three eighths of a *ratal* per head.[1] Of course, if there had been other articles of food available three eighths of a *ratal* would not have been too bad but there was nothing else ... no vegetables, no fruit, no meat or eggs or milk ... nothing at all. In place of eggs and milk we used to be given powder which you stirred into water to have something which at least looked like milk or beaten egg. The amount of powder available was very limited and it was almost as difficult to procure as gold dust. For countless generations bread has always been the staple food of the Maltese and the shortage of that commodity was a heavy burden to carry. Many were the instances of people paying ten shillings (then equivalent to about half a week's wages) for a fourpenny loaf of bread. I have heard stories of people giving away everything, including their honour, in return for food for themselves and their children.

Children of ten years and older, as I was, tend to have voracious appetites and it should be easy to imagine how hard it was for us to go to school morning after morning on an empty stomach. As I mentioned before, in the pre-war days my brother ate very little and regularly left half the food in his

94

plate but now when everybody was starving he used to lick the plate empty!

In the days when the food situation was at its most serious a merchant ship with a cargo of grain was sunk in the Grand Harbour and there were people who somehow managed to retrieve from the wreck sacks filled with wheat. When the sacks were opened up the stench of the wet grain was indescribable but that did not deter people facing starvation from making use of it for after drying the grain on rooftops they would grind it in the handmills normally used for grinding coffee beans. The flour was then made into spaghetti which were dried by spreading them over backs of chairs and then cooked. When the food was being shared around our eyes were on each other's plate to make sure that we were getting our proper share of the spaghetti.

When the food shortage became acute, communal kitchens, called Victory Kitchens, were introduced.[2] People were given coupons according to the number of persons in the family and each day at around noon people would queue up carrying plates and pots to get their portions. After so many years I cannot pronounce myself on the quality of the food produced by the Victory Kitchens but I can certainly say that we never left a crumb on our plates … except on one unforgettable occasion: the day when the Kitchens served green liver. At the time liver was considered to be a delicacy but in spite of hunger pangs nobody dared eat that kind of greyish green liver. People were furious and began to crowd round the Kitchen personnel brandishing the containers with the stew. The next instant they started throwing the contents at the Kitchen supervisor and staff, and within a few minutes the protest had turned into a riot, the only time during the war, I believe, that the Maltese rioted.

I need hardly say that the Victory Kitchen menu was very limited in its variety: vegetable soup, beans, thin broth, sardines and herrings more or less says it all. Surprisingly, though, in spite of so many hardships the Maltese never lost their sense of humour which often manifested itself in comic songs and sketches about topical items such as for instance about the military, the conscription, Hitler, Mussolini and Churchill and, as may be expected, the Victory Kitchens. One of the songs I remember being sung went thus in the vernacular:

Minestra u għaġin,	Soup and spaghetti,
Fażola u sardin,	Beans and sardines,
Tal-Victory Kitchen.	That's the Victory Kitchen.
Tawna l-Istrina,	We've had our Christmas presents,
Fażola u sardina,	Beans and a sardine,
Tal-Victory Kitchen.	That's the Victory Kitchen.
Bl-imgħarfa f'idejhom,	With ladle in hand,
Bil-cutex f'dufrejhom,	With cutex on fingernails,
Tal-Victory Kitchen.	That's the Victory Kitchen.
Saqajhom ħoxnin,	Solid stout legs,
Għax jieklu l-għaġin,	From eating spaghetti,
Tal-Victory Kitchen.	That's the Victory Kitchen.

There was little then to send you into fits of laughter but much to irritate you. One morning I woke up feeling pangs of hunger such as I never felt before and between bouts of sobbing informed my mother that I would not be going to school. At that precise moment an old woman, a neighbour of ours, happened to hear my sobs and wanted to know the reason for my crying. My mother told her the whole story. The old woman walked away only to return a few minutes later with a large round of bread. "Here", she said, "give this to your son; I could not bear to hear him cry. Poor child, who could ever imagine that matters would come to this stage when innocent children are denied the blessings of the Lord?" I went to school carrying the bread and when, during the break, I took it out and started munching it the other children crowded round me as if I was some kind of freak. A few of them begged me to give them a mouthful but, to my utter shame which even now gives me a feeling of guilt, I did not give away a morsel.

The one I have just recounted was by no means an isolated incident; we went to bed hungry and woke up hungry. I recollect occasionally going to the square at Raħal Ġdid to try and buy a carob bean or two from the owner of one of the *karozzini* which had by now begun to re-appear on the streets. For the same price, a penny, we could buy a couple of roasted beans before these were sold out.

Hunger inevitably leads to thieving which the authorities tried hard to prevent by giving harsh sentences for what we would now consider to be minor infractions, such as stealing a tin of corned beef. One episode comes to my mind here: through his contacts with sailors at the Dockyard my father occasionally managed to get hold of some item of foodstuff to supplement the meagre rations doled out to the family; this would be something like a packet of biscuits or a bar of chocolate the taste of which, in that time of shortages, we had almost forgotten. On such occasions my father would be in the seventh heaven, his eyes shining at the prospect of handing out the goodies to us. On the day in question as soon as he stepped into the house we realized that something was very wrong. His eyes were downcast and his face was pallid. He told my mother that during the night shift, as the tugboat on which he worked was lying alongside a merchantman, his mates were given a few bars of chocolate by the crewmen of that vessel. At that precise moment members of the Dockyard police force went on board and found the chocolate hidden away in the pockets of my father's mates. They were summarily arrested, arraigned before a court and sentenced to two years' imprisonment each. These respectable family men who had been risking their lives daily in their line of duty and whose only crime was to obtain a few sweets for their children found themselves out of a job, shorn of their civil rights. One might justify this by saying that the law is there to be observed in every detail and those who break it have to face the consequences; that line of reasoning may be perfectly correct but when one remembers the circumstances of those abnormal times one is bound to come to a different conclusion. The Draconian laws were meant to discourage pilferage of foodstuffs and the fact that people were resorting to theft of this nature to keep starvation off did not count as an extenuating circumstance before the courts. The punishment was without a shadow of doubt excessively harsh and totally disproportionate to the crime. Nowadays when one looks back at those days one cannot help experiencing a feeling of rage at such injustices when a man is thrown into prison and his family into dire straits simply for stealing a tin of corned beef normally worth a few pennies. Perhaps the reality becomes more palatable when one remembers that those were abnormal times and the common good required abnormal deterrents.

One of the depots for the storage of foodstuffs was located in the primary school at Raħal Ġdid and the tight security around the building can easily be imagined. But children, especially hungry children, are not easily put off by any security measure. In fact there was a gang of daredevil youngsters which regularly lay in wait for the loaded lorries to rumble up the road to the school, and then jump on to the truck; with incredible dexterity they would use sharp penknives to rip through a couple of sacks so that quantities of tins of condensed milk and other foodstuff would be scattered on the road. The youngsters would then carry the loot to one or another of two notorious black market dealers who would buy the tins for a shilling apiece or exchange them for cigarettes.

Dealers in the black market began to mushroom all over the place, selling at exorbitant prices items like flour, tinned milk, cigarettes and so on. Although there was a shortage of practically everything, there was comparatively speaking a lot of money in hand and some people could afford to buy commodities at a hundredfold the normal, peacetime price. The black marketeers were household names to the villagers; perhaps the most notorious of the dealers in the Raħal Ġdid area was a woman popularly known as "Ċetta tad-Dudu", who achieved the distinction of being mentioned by name in a book about Malta written by an Englishman. This Ċetta soon became the subject of a song which enjoyed great popularity among the Maltese; although the words were in Maltese few of those who sang it really understood the import of the words. I suspect that if people knew precisely what the real meaning was they would not have sung it so often. The song had nothing to do with the blackmarket!

The main door of the school which was being used as a depot did not quite reach down to the bottom and left a gap through which a very slim boy – a common species in those days – could squeeze with a little effort. One day I asked a boy who was thinner than me to squeeze through the gap into the school and once inside to draw one of the boxes to the door where I could then reach it. I put my hand through and levered off the lid. The box was packed with dried fruit and word soon got round that I was handing out dried fruit for free. All the neighbours trooped up to get their share and in next to no time the fruit had disappeared. I felt the urge to repeat the exploit but apparently the police had been alerted to similar thefts for I noticed that the number of watchmen had been increased and the gap under the door was closed up by raising the doorstep.

When you are hungry you tend to become reckless and to throw caution to the wind; this becomes even more true if you happen to be a lively youngster. It was such recklessness that led me and another boy to a prank that could easily have ended with dire consequences. Some distance from where we lived was a half-demolished block of houses in the yard of one of which grew a grapevine with fruit which had not yet ripened. Half starved as we were we used to go to this place and cut a bunch or two of sour grapes to relieve our hunger. This went on for some time until one day the owner caught us red-handed as we munched the hard grapes; my friend and I were terrified especially when he threatened to beat us with his bunch of heavy keys and to throw us into the well. On getting back home I was to get another shock for there waiting on the doorstep was a police sergeant who was asking for me. My mother was equally shocked and when I recounted my part of the story was far from relieved. As the police sergeant departed our mothers hurried to talk to the owner of the house and after making repeated apologies offered to make good any damages caused by their sons. But the owner would not accept apologies or offers. He must have been convinced that what we did was out of spite and that we had meant to cause damage to his property and he was in no mood to mete out forgiveness to the two of us. My mother however was not the sort to give up easily and a few days later approached the owner again and intimated to him that my friend was very ill as a result of the threats which he, the owner, had made and which had had a traumatic effect on the boy. Of course, all this was nothing more than a story which my mother had made up, her final tactics after all else had failed. Surprisingly my mother's story had the desired effect and the whole matter came to an end, though I must say that as far as I was concerned the prank left me with a sour taste for a long time afterwards.

In this day and age you would never imagine that walking around with a couple of tins of milk was a risky business because you ran a good chance of being pounced upon and relieved of your precious tinned milk. Things like that were a common occurrence during the war and my family went through one such experience. One evening as the darkness was falling, my brother Josie and I were walking from Gudja to Raħal Ġdid along the main road which led from Tarxien to Bir-id-Deheb. In the basket which we were carrying was the week's rations: two packets of milk powder, egg powder, some sugar, some flour ... a load which we in those days regarded as being worth its weight in gold. Partly because of the late hour and partly because of the fear of being caught in an air raid we were almost running. We little suspected that danger was coming from another quarter. From behind a rubble wall a boy of fourteen or fifteen suddenly appeared and as he approached we could see that his eyes were firmly fixed on the basket we were carrying. Without a word he handed us a couple of lemons which he was carrying and as we stood dumbfounded at this unexpected gesture, he grabbed the basket and dashed off as fast as his legs could carry him. We tried to give chase but there was no hope of catching up on him. At that instant there appeared an English soldier who quickly realized that we were chasing the older boy and gave chase too. With his long legs the soldier did not take long to overtake the youngster and soon managed to grab him by the scruff of the neck. The youngster, hoping to get out of the scrape turned to the soldier and said, "They grifty me the lemon, they grifty me the lemon!" At that time, the word "grifty" was understood by both Maltese and English to mean "steal". The soldier obviously did not believe him and after grabbing the basket out of his grasp gave him a parting kick on his bottom. The soldier, a heaven sent angel if ever there was one, then handed back the basket to us. We thanked the soldier as best we could and hurried home, glad to have been able to deliver the basket back home safely. That was certainly one of our lucky days for even to this day I am at a loss to imagine how I could have faced my mother with empty hands.

It was not only foodstuffs that were in short supply; there were also shortages of clothes and footwear. I remember some traders manufacturing shoes with uppers made of coarse cloth or canvas and soles made of rope or car tyres. The soles were also sometimes made of wood. Necessity is the mother of invention and substitutes had to be found for practically everything.

In the same way that coupons were issued which could be exchanged for food, there were coupons for clothing. People used to buy curtain cloth or woollen blankets which were then made into coats and other items of apparel. Wherever one looked one could see people dressed in that way. Clothes and shoes which had been put away years before were taken out of old boxes and worn again ... everything that could be used again was utilized.

As the war was coming to a close, goods of all sorts, such as clothing and toys began to pour in, sent by various organizations, mostly of Maltese settlers abroad who wanted to show their solidarity and appreciation with the local population which had been through so many tribulations and shortages and whose morale was at a low ebb. You could see interminable queues lining up at the door of the Protection Office hoping to get something useful ... a shirt, a pair of trousers, a pair of shoes, anything was welcome. Many of us who were still children naturally had their eyes mostly on the toys and managed to take home some toy. I remember some of my friends getting blocks and plasticine which none of us had ever seen before but unfortunately I was one of the disappointed few who was turned away empty-handed.

Food shortages were at their worst in August of 1942. You could see emaciated people wherever you looked, with bones showing through their skins; men tightened belts and women did the same to dresses. I recollect hearing people say that goats were being slaughtered for consumption and there were even rumours going about that cats and dogs were likewise being killed for the same purpose. I am inclined to believe now that these rumours were groundless, but I can certainly say that the situation was so desperate that rumours of that kind had no effect on people facing starvation. Fortunately half way through the month, on the feast day of the Assumption of the Blessed Virgin Mary, the convoy sailed into the Grand Harbour[3] and saved the population; the convoy subsequently became known as the Santa Marija Convoy. I do not remember the welcome given to the relief force as the convoy entered harbour but I certainly remember that within days of its arrival white flour made its appearance in the form of the white loaf which soon replaced the dark brown ration loaf. On first seeing a white loaf I could scarcely believe my eyes … God's grace had now descended on us after a long time of shortages and terror.

Notes and references

1. In May 1942 the bread ration was further reduced to three-eighths of a *ratal*. In the worst stretch of the food shortages, August 1942, the weekly rations consisted of:

    BREAD: three-eighths of a *ratal* (per day) [Note 1 *ratal* = 28 grams]

    RICE: not available

    SUGAR: not available

    BUTTER AND LARD: one person, a fourth of a *ratal*; four people or more, one *ratal*

    CORNED BEEF: two persons, one tin; 3 to 5 persons, two tins; 10 or more, four tins

    COOKING OIL: not available

    COFFEE: 4 to 5 persons, half *ratal* (Coffee was sold in the form of raw beans which we had to roast and then grind at home)

    CHEESE: 5 to 6 persons, half *ratal*; 13 or more: one *ratal*. (C.J. Boffa)

2. Victory Kitchens were introduced in the early months of 1942. These kitchens were established in every locality. The Kitchens used to prepare and serve soups, pasta, goat meat stew, *balbuljata* (a traditional simple Maltese dish), potatoes and similar cheap food. One of the principal aims of the Victory Kitchens was to economize on coal, matches, and paraffin which would have been used in much greater quantities if each family cooked for itself. The Kitchens were run entirely by Maltese personnel both as regards cooking and distribution. Each person was entitled to one coupon per day which could be exchanged for one portion. In addition to the regular staff, there was a number of "lady visitors" coming from well-known and respected families whose role was to pay surprise visits to the Kitchens to check on hygiene, food preparation and the size of the portions.

3. The Santa Marija Convoy (officially code-named *Operation Pedestal*): In August of 1942, Malta's food supplies were virtually exhausted; it was estimated that the stocks would only last a couple of weeks. To counter the threat of starvation a convoy of 14 merchant ships, laden with food, fuel and other essentials, fought its way from Gibraltar to the Island, escorted by a strong force of Royal Navy warships. The Germans were aware that the convoy would give a fresh lease of life to the besieged defenders and vowed to destroy the convoy before it reached the Malta harbours. The Germans came close to achieving their aims: nine of the cargo ships were sunk along with units of the escorting ships including the aircraft carrier HMS *Eagle*. Of the five cargo ships which made it to port between August 13-15, four were badly damaged. The oil tanker *Ohio* had her steering gear smashed and had to be lashed to two destroyers, one on either side, for the last part of the voyage. The arrival of the convoy was greeted with great enthusiasm from the huge crowds lining the vantage points in the Grand Harbour. Prayers of thanksgiving to God and the Virgin Mary, whose feast day was being celebrated on that date, were said in every village and town.

CHAPTER 11

The game resumes

As I have written in a previous chapter, the games we played during the troubled war years were but a reflection of the life that the Maltese people had become accustomed to. We did not have the toys and games that today's children have in abundance; we did not have footballs or comics and other books and, as I need hardly say, television, which was still unheard of in the early 1940's. Our games were inspired by what we saw around us: fighting and soldiers. The many regiments stationed in Malta during the war years came from several different parts of the United Kingdom as one could easily tell by the regimental names.[1] There were also Jewish soldiers clearly recognizable by the Star of David which was painted on their lorries, North African troops, black soldiers from Basutoland with their distinctive wide-brimmed hats ... While in Gudja the regiments were quartered in tents, those in Raħal Ġdid were billeted in various privately owned houses which had been requisitioned by the military authorities.

Our heroes in those years were the soldiers and we observed their drill routines and their every action so that we could play the part in our games. Occasionally we had the opportunity to enter the soldiers' quarters and be lucky enough to be given a cup of tea or a packet of biscuits or a few portions of chocolate which not only served to relieve the pangs of hunger but also made us feel privileged and in a different class from others. When we managed to reach that status in the hierarchy of children, the other boys would often beg us to be allowed into the quarters which gave us the chance to feel a certain degree of importance especially when we would refuse them entry saying, "Sorry! Sergeant's orders not to let anyone in!"

When we were with the rest of the boys and away from the soldiers' billets we would spend hours playing at soldiers, making our quarters in the bombed-out buildings which could be found in practically every street. Each street had its own "regiment" corresponding, I guess, to what nowadays we would call "gangs"; each "regiment" would have as its base a room constructed out of the stones of bombed houses, roofed over with "angle iron" or an iron bedstead salvaged from the ruins and covered with metal sheets or parts of doors and windows. We were tremendously proud of our "regimental" room which drew us like a magnet during holidays and Saturdays and on every conceivable occasion; hours would be spent in cleaning and improving the room, which to us was like a palace.

Once inside that room, we felt somehow that we were special and different from the other boys who congregated in other rooms, it gave us a feeling of belonging and when occasionally we were attacked by one of the other regiments we defended that room with every means at our disposal. Frequently, one of the neighbouring "regiments" would attack us and try to destroy that room and take our possessions. On such occasions we would take the necessary defensive action and before you could count up to ten we would be engaged in a battle with the opposing forces with stone throwing being the main weaponry. It was not a pleasant experience when you got in the way of a flying stone as I learnt at first hand on one such occasion. In that episode I was hit on the side of my head, just above the ear and I can still remember how painful that was. I cannot say I was surprised because that was precisely what was to be expected from engaging in "warfare".

The possibility of our room being attacked during the hours of darkness was what we most feared for then we would not be there to keep away the invaders and we could not imagine a worse scenario than our room ransacked and in ruins, to our young eyes a more terrible sight than seeing a whole town devastated! Our "Commanding Officer" Paddy used to dabble in electrics and he used to boast that he had found a system by which the "barbed wire" surrounding our room could be electrified His device was simplicity itself: a wire connecting the "barbed wire" to a doorbell. We were so convinced that the system worked and that anybody daring to cross the barbed wire would get a nasty surprise that none of us could summon enough courage to touch the wire. What counted most, of course, was that the "enemy" had come to know about the system and as a result kept their distance from our stronghold. From then on I could rest my head on the pillow every night without having to worry about some night attack on our room; no longer would I have to run to the balcony first thing in the morning to check that the room was still standing! My aunt had often asked me to tell her why I used to dash to the balcony as soon as I opened my eyes. I knew that she did not quite approve of my playing in our stronghold so I would reply that it was simply to see what the weather was like. Apparently, my aunt believed my story and went round telling the neighbours that her nephew was an astronomer in the making.

There were boys who had their quarters in bombed out buildings; such quarters, unlike ours which were built up stone on stone, had the advantage of being able to resist any attempt to bring them down. But there was another possibility open to us: we could ransack the place and carry off whatever could be lifted. On one occasion I raided one such place and as a reward for my enterprise was promoted to sergeant and decorated with three stripes; the episode, however, had an unhappy aftermath as I shall describe. One of the "regiments" had its headquarters in a bombed out house somewhere halfway between Raħal Ġdid and Tarxien. I had a long standing wish to mount a single-handed raid on one of the enemy's positions and to carry off some booty to show off to the rest of the boys. The enterprise was not an easy one to carry out successfully for this particular place was constantly guarded. I kept a close watch on the place, biding the time for the right moment to strike.

At last the opportunity was presented when the guard left his post for some time and I could enter the enemy quarters. Noiselessly I went up to the bathroom, which, it seemed, was the regiment's conference room. My eyes fell on a fairly large wooden box which contained forks and knives, a couple of plates, a few crown corks, some cartridges and some potatoes. I lifted the box and walked gingerly down the half-ruined staircase and out into the street, clutching the box and headed straight to our C.O., Paddy. As I expected Paddy was delighted with my prize and promoted me to the rank of sergeant awarding me the three stripes in the form of three crown corks stuck to my left sleeve. My happiness, however, was destined to be short lived for soon after my exploit I started having pangs of conscience when I realized that I was in reality guilty of stealing someone else's property.

Came the following Saturday when as usual I went to the church in the afternoon for confession. The confessor was Father F. and I told him about the stolen box. Father F. did not treat this as a childish prank at all and sternly told me that I had to return the stolen goods; he explained to me that his absolution was conditional on my returning every item of my booty. I was shattered! I was now scared that if I ventured to the enemy's quarters with the box I would run the risk of a severe beating and I struggled to find a way of returning my ill-gotten booty without taking a beating. Finally, I had an inspiration: I would recruit J.C.'s assistance. J.C. was the bully of the neighbourhood and when I explained to him my predicament he immediately agreed to help. "Don't worry", he said, "Get the box. I'll come with you and you can be sure nobody will dare as much as touch you." Sheepishly I went up to Paddy and told him the facts of the story and my determination to return the box. Paddy was understandably surprised at my statement but agreed to let me have the box back. I grabbed the box and trembling from head to foot made my way to the enemy's position with my new-found bodyguard at my side. As the two of us went into the house we saw about half a dozen boys looking menacingly at me. J.C. spoke briskly. "Someone stole this box and is returning it now. The matter is closed and I do not want to hear a word about it." I was on tenterhooks all the while and I was really glad to walk out of enemy territory unharmed and in one piece. As we walked back I thanked J.C. and made a resolution that I would never do such a thing again even if there were a hundred tempting promotions in sight.

The abundance of ruined houses – whole blocks of them – roofless, with walls blown in and mounds of stones wherever you cast your eyes provided us with plenty of opportunities to play our dangerous games. We literally had the freedom to enter and use countless ruins, a kind of freedom which cost the life of one of my friends when some roofing slabs gave way under his feet and he crashed down a couple of storeys. To this day I cannot understand how we did not have many such accidents when we were spending so much time among ruins. I feel sure that somebody up there was watching over us during those hazardous hours.

As I mentioned earlier our games were inspired by what was happening around us; we were compelled to copy whatever we observed. Once Josie and I decided to perform, or rather get somebody to perform, one of the stunts which we often saw pilots go through. The idea was to lower my younger brother Mario by "parachute" from the balcony to the ground. Before we embarked on the exploit we agreed to carry out a trial. We made him put on an old raincoat, then tucked a pillow under his left arm and another under his right arm, and after tying a rope around his waist we lowered him from the landing inside the house. The experiment, we agreed, was successful and we could go on to the real performance. We waited until our mother was out of the house and then instructed our brother to prepare himself for the attempt which, this time, would take place from the balcony. Our brother was evidently not looking forward to the performance; I noticed that his face had suddenly gone pale. He began to protest but we were bigger and he did not stand a chance. His teeth rattled as we began to lower him down gently from the balcony. He was already half way down when the rope slipped out of our hands and he hit the ground with a resounding thud. One of the neighbours who saw all this ran to look for my mother and when she found her told her the whole story. My mother, boiling with anger, screamed at us, "How could you do that? You could have killed your brother! How could you?". But we were still immature boys who did not pause to consider the consequences of our actions. Those were times of war and we were exposed to daily experiences of death and destruction and by then we had grown used to that kind of life.

It still remains a mystery to me how we daily tempted fate and yet, by some sort of miracle, lived to tell the tale. To give one instance: in the summer of 1942 some youths discovered a new way of passing the time, sending up real rockets into the sky. While these youths were walking along the foreshore at Marsa they noticed that some lighters moored to the wharf were loaded with large cartridges some one and a half feet in height and with a diameter of about four or five inches. The cartridges were packed with cordite, which when triggered off with the detonator or "caps", as we used to call it, caused the explosion which shot off the warhead. The cordite sticks had the thickness of a cigarette cork tip and had five holes running down the whole length. Oblivious to the risks involved the youths would remove the sticks from the cartridge, then pack them tight into empty cans and insert a lighted cigarette into the container. The effect was instantaneous: the contraption would shoot up into the sky with a loud bang and flashes of light like *festa* rockets. On some occasions even adults would join in to enjoy the fireworks. The fun did not last long thanks to the police force which put an end to the free show; with hindsight I realise that the police action must have saved many a young man's life for we were literally playing with fire.

In those days, there were plenty of safety catches around; these were simple mechanical devices mounted on rifles. The catches had a very strong spring and we used to enjoy producing loud clicks by pressing the right parts. Some boys, however, were not content with simply producing noise and they would use the catches to fling lead bullets into the air and then, if you were unlucky enough to get one of the bullets on your head you would be "king". On the whole the game was apparently harmless for I do not remember any of the boys ever being injured in the process.

Rifle bullets had the same shape as the shells used by the anti-aircraft guns, but much smaller – about an inch and a half long and made of lead with a silvery metal cover. There were so many of these bullets around that we used to play with them as, in better days, we used to play with toys and marbles and, especially around the feast of St Martin, with nuts. One game we used to enjoy was standing up a number of bullets in a straight line and then taking those we were able to knock down. Sometimes the game would take another form: we would draw a small square on the ground, each of us would put, say, three or four bullets in the square and then take turns to try and knock out of the square as many as possible to take as winnings. Because of their cylindrical shape the heavy bullets were not as easy to knock out of the square as marbles or nuts in a similar game.

Besides the risks associated with explosives there were risks from other quarters. I remember one incident which could have had serious consequences, possibly fatal, that occurred one July day in 1943.

It so happened that on that day the Bishop was due to administer the sacrament of Confirmation to the children who were then living in rock-cut shelters in the dry moat encircling Birgu; the ceremony was to be conducted in a cleared part of the severely damaged parish church of St Lawrence. No altar boys could be found to help in the proceedings and the only priest available was the archpriest of the parish. My brother, myself and another boy were known to have a cassock and surplice and so the three of us were asked to participate in what was to be a very plain unassuming ceremony. The rite took place as planned and as soon as we were freed from our duties the three of us decided to go straightaway to Rinella creek for a swim. As was to be expected in those days the small beach was deserted, and in a few minutes we were thoroughly enjoying ourselves in the warm waters a stone's throw away from Bighi naval hospital. But luck was against us. Suddenly a large number of North African soldiers trooped out of nearby Fort Ricasoli and took to the water. One of the soldiers struck up a conversation with us and we spent some time trying to find words which were common to the Maltese and Arabic languages. Suddenly, without warning, our newly found friend grabbed my brother and shoved his head under the water and held it there. My brother somehow managed to wriggle out of the man's stranglehold. We quickly grabbed our clothes and, shaking with fear, took to our heels. Our trip to Rinella had almost ended in tragedy.

Notes and references

1. During the war there were 11 British regiments stationed in Malta: the *Manchester Regiment*, the *Royal Irish Fusiliers*, the *Royal East Kent*, the *Queen's Own Royal West Kent*, the *Devonshire Regiment*, the *Dorset Regiment*, the *King's Own Royal Regiment*, the *Lancashire Fusiliers*, the *Cheshire Regiment*, the *Royal Hampshire Regiment* and the *Durham Light Infantry* as well as *Royal Artillery Regiments* and other units such as the *Royal Engineers*, and the *Royal Army Service Corps*.

CHAPTER 12

Peace returns

I attended Raħal Ġdid Primary School for just one year,
in the class which prepared us to sit for the Lyceum Entrance
Examination. My classmates and I were lucky in having as our
teacher Mr Spiteri in whose eyes the pupils predominated
over everything else. He was so dedicated to his work that
he used to be at school by quarter past seven when lessons
were supposed to start at eight and he rarely left the premises
before five or half past five. He was so keen to make us learn
that sometimes he applied the cane too freely and treated us
very harshly. Once I had the terrifying experience of being
grabbed by the throat and almost throttled simply because at
some moment my attention wandered from the blackboard;
his behaviour, although patently well meant, often verged on
the violent and brought parents' wrath on his head.

In telling my story I have been careful to tell it as it happened,
without glossing over embarrassing occasions and without
exaggerating or omitting experiences. I can honestly say here,
especially to my young readers, that to me schooling was very
important. Like any other child of my age, I loved games and
sports but I never neglected my lessons or let play interfere
with them with the result that I tended to do well at school. I am
not emphasizing this to cut a fine figure with my readers but

merely to present, as completely as possible, a picture of myself and of the experiences I lived through in those dark days which we have come to call the Second Great Siege.

Apart from that incident when Mr Spiteri almost throttled me, I do not recall any similar behaviour on his part towards me. With two or three other pupils I was the apple of his eye and provided him with the satisfaction of seeing a return for his efforts to make us learn at any cost. Those few of us were the kind of children a teacher would like to have in the class especially on those occasions when a class inspection was in progress and we were able to answer most of the questions which the inspector had in store for us.

Mr Spiteri was one of the best teachers that I remember and when I later became a teacher myself my respect for him remained. For him, teaching was not just another job, but a mission which demanded total dedication. Even when he was obviously sick, with red eyes and a hoarse voice, he would still come to do his daily stint at school. If he could be faulted on any point it was his total determination that his pupils would learn the day's lesson. When, as sometimes happened, the pupil failed to respond to his teaching, he just could not accept the situation and would vent his anger on the unfortunate boy. Such behaviour did not make him popular with pupils and parents and more than once he clashed with the latter and with his superiors such as the head of school and the inspectorate.

In November 1942 Carmelo Borg Pisani was hanged at the Corradino Prisons. Borg Pisani was an idealist who, some six months before, had been apprehended after a clandestine landing in Malta on a mission to obtain and relay to the Fascist Government certain military intelligence ahead of the projected invasion by Italian and German forces. I had not heard about the matter before the day of his execution, that is, November 28; in fact the local papers, the *Times of Malta*

116

and *Il-Berqa*, had kept silent and did not publish the story. However, as we all know, Malta has never been the place where a secret is safe. In a small island where everybody knows everybody else the word soon got round that a spy had been apprehended and given a capital sentence by a court made up of three judges. (The jury system was suspended during the war.) Somehow my brother got to know all the details about the date and time when the execution was to be carried out and with one of his friends he had made up his mind to go to have a look. The Corradino prisons are close to the centre of Raħal Ġdid, a stone's throw from the parish church near which we lived.

When an execution was about to take place strict precautions were always taken and few people had the "privilege" to be present during the carrying out of this cruel sentence, a barbarous practice even though there are some who maintain that it is necessary. As a boy of twelve, my brother Josie was not the one to take no for an answer and the appointed time saw him and his friend perched on a wall from where they could observe the funeral procession wending its way from the prison to the cemetery. This would have been around nine o'clock in the morning, about an hour and a half after the hanging which is recorded as having taken place at thirty four minutes past seven. According to regulations in such executions the body had to be left hanging for an hour at the expiry of which it would be examined by the medical team and then buried. November 28 happened to fall on a Saturday and so my brother did not have to attend school.

My brother was struck by the procession with the corpse which he had witnessed and on getting back home proceeded to recount all that he had seen that morning. A few days after this episode my brother was in bed with a high fever and fell into a delirious state. He began to mutter words about the procession and to sing snatches of the hymns that were sung.

117

The whole episode made such an impression on me that when I grew up, many years later, I made up my mind to get to know more about the unique incident in Malta during the Second World War.

It was during this year that, in addition to the sufferings which we had been subjected to, there loomed another calamity which struck a number of families and terrorized the whole population. In the last few months of 1942 there was an outbreak of polio or "paralysis" as we used to call it in those days.[1] Those struck by the disease were maimed for life, generally in the lower limbs. As the disease was contagious schools were closed down as a precaution. I think I can safely say without fear of contradiction that my generation experienced every imaginable tribulation during the five years of the war.

The weeks and months in my class rolled on swiftly and by that time the war had receded from our shores even though there were still two years to go before its official conclusion. In June, or it could have been July, we took our examinations for entry to the Lyceum; many of us managed to pass though we were competing with boys two or three years older. The age at which you could take the examinations in that year had been raised to fourteen presumably to give a chance to those pupils who because of the war had had their schooling disturbed.

A month after the written examinations, those of us who had been successful were asked to attend for the oral examination to be held in Valletta. We were at the appointed place at about nine when we were told that we would have to wait for quite some time before our turn came up. Around noon we went again to the same place and once again we were told that we would not be called before the late afternoon. There were no buses running at the time and as we had not brought any food with us, we were feeling hungry. We had to do something. One of us had a brilliant idea: we could each fork out threepence and with the money buy some food from the market in Merchants Street. There were four of us and the money at our disposal amounted to a shilling which at that time was quite a modest sum. After some consultation between us we decided to buy some tripe and half a loaf and then we went into the courtyard at the Palace where under the watchful eye of the statue of Neptune we consumed our food.

My turn to go in for the oral came at about four. I duly answered the questions to the best of my knowledge and then walked all the way to Raħal Ġdid. Shortly after, my parents received a note stating that I had qualified for a place at the Lyceum. A decisive step in my life had been reached. The very fact that now I was in a secondary school gave me a sense of responsibility and unwittingly I gradually began to neglect the old friends, "the regiment", and to form new friendships.

What I believe severed the last link I had with "the regiment" was the theft of the only pair of shoes which I had at that time. As I have mentioned more than once in passing clothes and shoes were not simply scarce commodities; you had to spend a fortune to obtain things like that. The reader can imagine the cautions and warnings I received from my mother when, with superhuman efforts and at enormous cost, she managed to procure a pair of shoes for me. "Don't you dare play football in those shoes!" she would warn me time and time again. I was mature enough then to understand fully my mother's apprehensions and I was totally determined to take particular care of them. What I could never have foreseen, however, was the behaviour of one of my friends. We were playing among the ruins of bombed houses when I suddenly got the idea that my shoes would be getting some rough treatment on the rubble and thoughtfully removed them and tied them up on a branch of a pomegranate tree growing among the stones. No sooner had I turned my face than I realized with a shock that the shoes had disappeared. I turned every stone, looked behind each clump of grass, I searched every corner and finally asked each of my friends whether this was some sort of joke and to, please, hand them back. To cut a long story short the shoes were gone for ever and now the problem was how to face my mother! I had been so determined to look after my new shoes and I had promised my mother solemnly that I would do so and now they had vanished into thin air. My head felt as if it would burst; what was I to do? There was nothing I could do except return home and face the music. You can imagine the scene my mother made: I thought she would have a stroke and got doubly scared. In the midst of all this my father came home and in a flash joined in. He was even more furious than my mother and between them they made a scene I would never forget. There was no likelihood of my being given another pair of new shoes and in the end I had to be content with borrowing a pair from my brother who wore a size larger than me; still I had the consolation of being able to say that a pair of large shoes are better than none at all.

That ugly incident of the stolen shoes taught me an important lesson: now that I was in a secondary school I had to behave like a mature and responsible person. I felt I had to say goodbye to childish games and to friends I had played with for years. It seemed as if I had changed overnight. My childhood, with all its innocent joys and adventures, now lay behind and, at an earlier age than most of my friends, I was now a young man.

The war has been barely mentioned in these last few pages. With the arrival of the Santa Marija Convoy the spectre of starvation had faded away and as air raids petered out the war became almost a thing of the past especially for us youngsters. I do not know whether adults changed their attitudes; perhaps they followed the progress of the war in Europe and the Far East in news bulletins on radio and in the press. In those days even if newspapers were not as common as now the latest information about the war in its various theatres was never lacking. In Raħal Ġdid there was an establishment which served as an information centre with newspaper cuttings and photos pasted on its window panes giving the latest news ... the good news, I would think. The battles won by the Allies were naturally given prominence and when things went badly for them not a word ... I guess it was like that in every country. After all it is quite understandable that in a state of war the people's morale is as important as guns and bullets.

The information centre, the *Information Bureau*[2] as it was called then, attracted crowds of people all eager to know the latest from the fronts and when occasionally some victory for Britain or its Allies was announced the event would be celebrated with band marches and waving of banners. I remember the day when Mussolini was assassinated[3] the shop owner quickly made up a coffin and sent us boys marching with it through the streets of Raħal Ġdid. One can easily imagine the merriment with which we celebrated the death of this personality about whom and his confederate Hitler we had heard so much throughout our childhood.

Another memorable day for me was the one when my aunt took me with her to Valletta and I saw hundreds of people running around waving handkerchiefs. It was the king, George VI, the present queen's father, who was in Malta on a flying visit[4] and who just a year before had awarded the George Cross, the highest possible civil decoration, to the Island for the gallantry shown during the dark days of the siege. The simple fact that I had actually seen the King in flesh and blood made me happy because it immediately brought back to my mind memories of my first schooldays when one of the stories in our Maltese reading book described the great unforgettable moment when the hero had seen the King face to face.

When one is twelve, three or four years make up a third of one's life; for me at that age that meant living a third of my life in a state of war. I yearned for the day when peace would return. I remember as if it was yesterday how I used to try to imagine what life would be like in peacetime. I would try to conjure up images of being able to sleep through a whole night, of having as much food and sweets as I desired, of having toys ... but I simply could not visualize what life was like before the war.

However, even if by that time life had not yet returned to normality, things were on the whole much better than in the previous two years. The shop-windows gradually began to fill up with articles of food and clothing and more and more cars could be seen on the roads. Air raids had become a thing of the past and it was obvious that the war had receded from our shores.

The Christmas of 1944 was another red-letter day for me: I had once again been chosen to deliver the traditional boy's sermon. On that occasion I was naturally older; I could read well enough and did not need any coaching or to have my uncle by my side to prompt me if I stumbled over my lines; I first delivered the sermon at the Raħal Ġdid parish church at the conclusion of the usual procession held by members of the MUSEUM and then, after a short break at home, together with my uncle and brother hired a *karozzin* (horse-drawn cab) to take us to Gudja where I was to deliver the sermon for the second time. In that particular year the Mass was held at midnight, just like before the war, and although the war was not yet over one could easily imagine the angels singing 'peace to all men of good will'. I was very excited and happy to be back in the village where I had spent some two and a half years and where my family had been received with open arms.

Two and a half years are a big slice of a boy's life and I found things had changed a great deal. Most of the altar boys I had been friends with were no longer there and their place had been taken by unfamiliar faces. As I was putting on the vestments in the sacristy before going to deliver the sermon, I felt as if I was a stranger. But then, as soon as I had mounted the pulpit, I had the same feelings as of old, a feeling that I was an adopted son of the village.

Six months later Germany surrendered[5] and as far as Europe was concerned the war was, at long last, over. The news filled me with inexpressible happiness and my mind was at peace. Even at that young age I could understand the death and devastation which were always on our doorsteps and the risks we were running, day after day, of being bombed out of existence. Admittedly, people had in time somehow got used to the hardships of war for it is well known that the human being has the gift of being able to adapt to any situation no matter how difficult that may be. However, there was always indelibly marked at the back of one's mind the sheer terror which even now at my age I occasionally experience at night when I dream about bombs falling around me and burying me under the rubble or being chased by German soldiers firing their guns.

The scars that those times have left in me still bring up images in my mind of people being buried under the ruins of their homes, of the acrid smell of cordite, of starvation and scabies, of entire nights spent in deep, damp and cold shelters, of the wailing of sirens in the small hours, of ear splitting explosions and of intervals of sheer terror. The passage of time has softened some of those memories but it can never obliterate them for those experiences have become part of me, they are the inheritance which has been passed down to me and to those of my age from peoples thirsting for the blood of others during the dark years of the Second World War.

Notes and references

1. 415 were struck by the disease which killed 17. (Philip Vella: *Malta Blitzed but not Beaten.*)

2. The Principal Information Office charged with keeping the public informed was housed in a few rooms on the top floor of the Post Office. The top officials were British assisted by a number of Maltese employees. The Raħal Ġdid information centre, as well as those in other localities, were not officially designated as Information Offices.

3. Mussolini died on April 28, 1945. Together with his mistress, he was executed by a firing squad on being captured by the Partisans at Dongo, near Como, north Italy.

4. King George VI arrived in Malta on HMS *Aurora* on June 20, 1943 at about 10 in the morning. He was on the Island for only about 8 hours during which time he paid a visit to the Dockyard and the Three Cities. He was then driven through cheering crowds at Raħal Ġdid, Marsa, Ħamrun and Birkirkara. Malta was awarded the George Cross on April 15, 1942. The official presentation took place later on September 13 of the same year when the Chief Justice, Sir George Borg, received the award from the Governor, Lord Gort, on behalf of the Maltese people.

5. Germany capitulated on May 7, 1945. The terms of the unconditional surrender were signed at the Headquarters of General Eisenhower, the Supreme Commander of the Allied Forces in Europe. That marked the end of the war in Europe after almost six years of fierce fighting and millions of servicemen and civilians killed,. The war in the Pacific dragged on for a few more months when, after the dropping of two atom bombs on Hiroshima and Nagasaki the Japanese surrendered on September 2, 1945, thus officially bringing to an end the Second World War.

6. The Communist-dominated states of Eastern Europe cut off their links with Moscow in the late 1980s and early 1990s.

CHAPTER 13

The past and the years to come

Thirty years or more have passed and each one of us carries a store of memories, some sad, some happy, of the ups and downs which we lived through. In the minds of those who lived through those times recollections of the war are still vivid. Those of us who were young at the time will never forget the terrifying reverberations of explosions and the gruesome images of war which have indelibly carved themselves in our minds, at an age when we were still in the formative stages of our development. As a cleft in a tree trunk grows larger over the years instead of disappearing, so our memories have become clearer as we have grown older.

These days we can compare our upbringing with that of our children and can experience the pleasure of seeing them grow up in good health and in a prosperous world. At the same time we cannot obliterate our childhood memories of the misery and shortages which were part of our everyday life. When I observe the comfortable life our children are living, I cannot help remembering the hardships which we as children had to endure in those unhappy days.

But in a sense I do not envy them their comforts for I have the feeling that our children are reaping the fruits of our labours and of the tribulations of their fathers and mothers (and us as children) who suffered and toiled so that our country would remain free. Should the war have had a different ending, with the Allies on the losing side, the world in which we and our children live now would have been totally different.

As I have said in previous chapters, in spite of the fact that the war years were very hard for us and I still relive from time to time some of the terrible events in my dreams, I somehow feel that my life has been enriched by the experience. I realize, of course, that I am looking at those years in this light simply because the sheer terror, the insatiable hunger, the tormenting scabies, the whine of sirens, the reeking smell of cordite, the bodies buried under the rubble, the earth shuddering under my feet, are nothing more than memories and one can learn to live with them, however vivid and alive they may still remain. I should also say that I have some pleasant memories of the war. The years spent in Gudja and later on in Raħal Ġdid influenced in no small way the development of my character and my whole personality. In the months I spent running around with children of peasant stock I learnt a great deal about the realities of life and, even after the passage of many years, I feel grateful for having gone through the experience.

There was no place during the war for pampering and mollycoddling! We had of necessity to be content with whatever was available, little though that was. When I observe children and youngsters of these days losing their heads over trivial games, their energies directed towards trifling pursuits, I cannot help feeling that in a way we were more fortunate. When I read about the ways in which today's youngsters are seeking excitement that feeling becomes even stronger. In those distant years excitement was constantly in the air we breathed: airplanes engaged in deadly combat, pilots floating down under their parachutes, an enemy bomber caught in the beams of a searchlight on a dark night while anti-aircraft shells explode around it, such experiences were common and provided all the excitement one could hunger for.

I would not like to be misunderstood: I would be the last person to maintain that war is preferable to peace. The hardships which we endured in those days can never make any aspect of war desirable, but I have a vague feeling that what the war did not destroy is being eroded under our very eyes. The foundations on which our civilization has been built are being slowly but inexorably undermined in more ways than one. Though in these last thirty years we have been able to steer away from any major war, conflicts on a smaller scale are rampant in many parts of the globe, costing innumerable lives. Nations which fought with all their might to resist Nazi and Fascist dictatorships find themselves now in a worse predicament, dominated by Communism, and, thirty years after the fall of the Nazi and Fascist regimes, still await their freedom. It is sad to realize that in Eastern Europe the majority of people who were children during the war or who were born after the war do not know what it means to be free and have yet to experience the freedom for which millions of people gave up their lives.

True peace will never reign until the day when the human race understands that peace cannot be built on might and hatred but only on love and respect. Until that day dawns the outlook will be bleak indeed and the youth of tomorrow, like us children of yesteryear, will be doomed to live in a climate of fear and tension, of terror and destruction.

I can only hope that the future will be a different one.

Titles on Military History
at **Wise Owl** PUBLICATIONS

Malta at War   J. A. Mizzi / M. A. Vella   Lm1.85 (€4.31)
Malta's most comprehensive publication in words and pictures of the war years. Available in individual magazines or five softbound volumes (Lm24 [€55.90] each volume). Volume 5 will be available in 2008/9.

Battle of Grand Harbour 1941   Joe Caruana   Lm2.95 (€6.87)
A detailed account of the attack by the Italian Navy on the Grand Harbour.

Squadron 249 at Malta   Brian Cull / F. R. Galea   Lm4.95 (€11.53)
War diaries of Malta's top scoring fighter squadron.

Call Out   Frederick Galea   Lm8.95 (€20.85)
War time diary of air/sea rescue operations at Malta. The squadron successfully carried out a record of over 270 pick-ups throughout the war.

Guns of Ħaġar Qim   Stanley Fraser   Lm8.95 (€20.85)
A vivid account of the hazardous life of a Malta based gunner during World War Two.

War Scrawls   Joseph C. Attard   Lm1.95 (€4.54)
Diary of a Maltese soldier.

Women of Malta   Frederick R. Galea   Lm3.95 (€9.20)
Two ladies' accounts of the war years in Malta.

Wise Owl PUBLICATIONS
59, Levels 1 & 2, Main Street,
Rabat RBT1012, Malta GC, Europe
Tel: 2145 3303
E-mail: wiseowl@maltanet.net
Website: www.wiseowlmalta.com

Note: Please add 20% for overseas postage. Post free to Malta.